# VISITS TO THE OTHER SIDE

*A Series of Paranormal Events*

WILLIAM H. WESTBROOK, BASc

Victor:
May you have good health
and peace of mind

Bill

**Trafford**
PUBLISHING™

Order this book online at www.trafford.com/07-2277
or email orders@trafford.com

Most Trafford titles are also available at major online book retailers.

Note for Librarians: A cataloguing record for this book is available from Library
and Archives Canada at www.collectionscanada.ca/amicus/index-e.html

Printed in Victoria, BC, Canada.

ISBN: 978-1-4251-5197-3

*We at Trafford believe that it is the responsibility of us all, as both individuals
and corporations, to make choices that are environmentally and socially sound.
You, in turn, are supporting this responsible conduct each time you purchase a
Trafford book, or make use of our publishing services. To find out how you are
helping, please visit www.trafford.com/responsiblepublishing.html*

*Our mission is to efficiently provide the world's finest, most comprehensive
book publishing service, enabling every author to experience success.
To find out how to publish your book, your way, and have it available
worldwide, visit us online at www.trafford.com/10510*

 www.trafford.com

**North America & international**
toll-free: 1 888 232 4444 (USA & Canada)
phone: 250 383 6864 ♦ fax: 250 383 6804 ♦ email: info@trafford.com

**The United Kingdom & Europe**
phone: +44 (0)1865 722 113 ♦ local rate: 0845 230 9601
facsimile: +44 (0)1865 722 868 ♦ email: info.uk@trafford.com

10 9 8 7 6 5

# Contents

*Do not stand at my grave and weep,*
*I am not there, I do not sleep.*

*I am in a thousand winds that blow;*
*I am the softly falling snow.*
*I am the gentle showers of rain;*
*I am the fields of ripening grain.*

*I am in the morning hush,*
*I am in the graceful rush*
*Of beautiful birds in circling flight,*
*I am the star shine of the night.*

*I am in the flowers that bloom,*
*I am in a quiet room.*
*I am in the birds that sing,*
*I am in each lovely thing.*

*Do not stand at my grave and cry,*
*I am not there. I do not die.*

MARY ELIZABETH FRYE

# Acknowledgments

I have been blessed with unusual paranormal experiences that I would like to share with others; experiences that some will find hard to accept. As I describe them, try to suspend any disbelief and become an open-minded skeptic. While writing this book I have been favored by the assistance of friends on both sides of the veil between this world and the Other Side.

Without my mentor at Humber College, John Bentley Mays, this book would never have been written.

Here at home, the invaluable editing my ex-British friend, Ben Roberts, has provided is greatly appreciated.

Carol-Ann Bosley at the Ottawa Spiritualist temple has been most helpful. My thanks go as well to the platoon of people on the Other Side who have been encouraging and helping me to write about my unusual experiences. Foremost among these, my Spirit Guide, White Fox, has been a constant source of inspiration and encouragement, along with a Specialized Helper named Beulah, a flamboyant actress from the 1920's.

Over the past eight years I have received readings from three mediums, Jan Remington, Wendy James, Deborah Levin and an Ottawa Mystic Rene Beaupre, had three noteworthy dreams, identified three of my past lives worth pursuing with the help of three past life facilitators, and enlisted the aid of three travelers in the fifth dimension, namely Archangel

Rafael, the Angel of Healing, Eagle Starfire, a Blackfoot medicine man, and Isis an Egyptian Goddess that protect me, and help me send unconditional love to handicapped people.

The friendly people at Trafford Publishing, in Victoria, BC, provide me and my book exemplary service. Victor J. Crapnell, the award winning graphics designer, in Victoria, produced the book cover.

I.

# My Spiritual Background

My early exposure to religion was through the Presbyterian Church in Toronto. As a child, I, along with my younger brother and sister, regularly attended Sunday school, and often went to both the morning and evening services as well, held in the church at the end of our street. In 1946, upon returning to civilian life following World War II, I joined the Dr. A.S. Grant Bible Class, at the same church. Made up of about 75 young adults in their twenties we enjoyed getting together after class at the Panama, a Bloor Street restaurant, for Coconut Cream pie or a sundae. Later while living in the Montreal area, I served as Chairman of the Building Committee for a new church in Beaconsfield, using my project management skills to help select an architect and interface with the congregation. However, when I was asked to teach a Sunday school class of 10-year-old boys, I found the lessons provided were difficult to cover with conviction. That was the beginning of my recognition that I was more spiritual than religious. I felt that I could deal directly with God, without the middleman. Most of the middlemen I had been exposed to were less than inspiring. Now that I'm firmly planted in my senior years,

I can see that the spiritual path has been the calling of my soul for a long time, and I am ready to devote the rest of my life to walking it as best I can.

Following the War, during which I served in the RCAF, as a navigator on Lancaster bombers, I attended the University of Toronto and received my BASc in Electrical Engineering in 1951. As a Professional Engineer, a major Canadian tele-communications corporation employed me with offshore assignments in New Jersey and Virginia. I eventually retired in Ottawa, in 1983.

One day, early in 2000, I noticed in the paper that Sister Mangalam Lena was looking for volunteers to help her put together a non-profit organization whose mission was to provide spiritual care to those with no other means of spiritual support, so I phoned and offered my help. Sr. Mangalam is a Franciscan Missionary of Mary, and founder of Home-Based Spiritual Care. Born in Sri Lanka, I found her to be energetically dedicated to helping those who are confined to their homes; that may be lonely, chronically ill, elderly, terminally ill, or dying. At that time she was working from her small room in the Convent, but we were eventually able to have HBSC registered as a charity and find suitable office space. During the three years I was Secretary of the organization, and served on the Board of Directors, Sister Mangalam kept me supplied with choice teas from her native land, Sri Lanka.

While I was associated with Home-Based Spiritual Care, I would have liked to visit our clients who were terminally ill, but because of my lack of training this was not possible. Therefore, in the fall of 2005, with a view to obtaining such training. I joined a Friends of Hospice Volunteer Education Program. As the only man in a class of 12, I felt outnumbered, but Debbie Watt the instructor along with the other class members made me feel welcome. The Friends of

Hospice Ottawa is a registered charity dedicated to providing supportive hospice palliative care services. Hospice palliative care aims to relieve suffering and improve the quality of living and dying. The mission of the Friends is to support, educate and empower, those who are affected by, or are caring for, a loved one with a life-threatening illness. Their purpose is to care for these people and help them live as fully as possible.

Unfortunately, after only a few weeks a seizure put a temporary cramp in my plans, as this resulted in my driver's licence being canceled, and I had to drop out of the course. Now that I am able to drive again, I hope to continue where I left off.

Regarding my current views on God and religion, Deepak Chopra in *"How to Know God"* tells us that "Although it doesn't seem possible to offer a single fact about the Almighty that would hold up in a court of law, somehow the vast majority of people believe in God–as many as 96 percent, according to some polls."

I too believe in God, but I am not so sure about religion. I think that, in general, organized religion has done more harm than good. The Dalai Lama tells us that *"we should respect other religions... the essence of all religions is essentially the same: to achieve a true sense of brotherhood, a good heart, and respect for others."* If we can develop these qualities from within our heart, then he thinks we can achieve true peace. Unfortunately, that is a very big If.

As a Christian, my God is a God of Infinite, Unconditional Love. Because of the great love that God has for all humankind, he makes no distinction between the blessed soul of Christ and the lowliest of the souls that are to be saved regardless of their religion.

Soon after we pass over to the Other Side, we review the life we have just left. It's not God, and it's not our Angels or Spirit Guides that judge our just completed life; it's us. We judge ourselves, our humanity or lack of it, our acts of kindness and selfishness and most important, how well we accomplished the goals we set; before we started the life we have just left.

# First Visit

I am a skeptic by nature, and have not always believed that there are people who can communicate with the spirit world. So when my great friend Bill M. told me he thought it was possible to contact the Other Side, as a practicing electrical engineer, I was dubious. Bill was a bright, quiet, unassuming guy who grew up on a farm in Western Saskatchewan, and as an esteemed professional engineer, he was not prone to making rash statements. Sadly Bill passed over to the Other Side in the Salvation Army Hospital in Ottawa in 1983 but it wasn't until 1998, fifteen years after he passed over that I eventually decided to attend a Psychic Fair to see if I could reach him in some way. It wasn't until fifteen years after he passed over that I eventually decided to attend a Psychic Fair to see if I could reach him in some way.

At that time, I tended to regard the tarot card readers, astrologers and numerologists that frequent these events as well meaning, but misguided. So upon arrival at my first Psychic Fair, trying to be non-judgmental, I entered the hall and, on looking around, I saw people who seemed to be quite enthusiastic about what they were doing, however I felt out of place like a stranger in a new world that was foreign to me. There were a total of about sixty booths arranged in several long rows, representing a wide variety of special interests including: astrology, clairvoyant readings, afterlife communication, aura photography, herbal products and books. In one corner there was a Lecture Area with a sign listing upcoming talks on Angel Readings, Psychic Demos, Spirit Communication and Tarot Cards. As I looked around, my attention was drawn to a middle-aged, motherly woman, who already had several people waiting at her table. Beside her was a small sign stating she was a Clairvoyant and Medium by the name of Jan Remington. I approached her booth and when my turn came, explained that I was new at this, but hoped to contact my friend, Bill. She then proceeded to take me on my first Visit to the Other Side. It seemed as though Bill was waiting there, wondering what took me so long, because Jan had no difficulty contacting him. Here, at last, was confirmation of my friend's belief. It was wonderfully exciting to be able to communicate with him. Through Jan, he told me that I would know when he comes around because I would have an itchy nose. Also during the Reading, he told Jan that I was one of those lucky guys that always seemed to come out on top. Regrettably, before he passed over, I was unable to spend as much time with Bill as I would have liked, but I knew how he felt about contacting the Other Side. In my frequent subsequent visits, he is always there. He tells me that when I am driving he is usually in the back seat of my car, and he always hears me when I speak to him.

Years ago, when we lived in the Montreal area, Bill and I were Great Books discussion leaders. We would meet with friends who agreed that there are few activities more pleasurable than reading and talking about books that matter. When I asked him, through Jan, if he had read any good books lately, he recommended "*Conversations With God*", by Neale Donald Walsch. He said that although our past reading had included the Old Masters, like Socrates and Plato, now there were new writers to explore, which meant we have much more to learn. Bill invited any questions I might have and pointed out that by using clairaudience we could keep in touch. I had not heard the term before, but clairaudience means "clear hearing." A medium like Jan can hear the higher frequency spirit voices and let me know what she hears. Telling me that I have a lot of writing to do, Bill suggested, that I find a quiet place and start writing inspirational messages. I was not sure what he had in mind. I should have asked for clarification.

At that first session, I also discovered that there was someone else there who wanted to contact me. It was "Buddy" a Cocker Spaniel puppy that I had years ago. Buddy admitted that he had been a difficult pet that was hard to get near, and apologized for giving my family and me, a hard time.

Another one of Jan's gifts comes under the heading of Psychometry. Using an object, such as, a ring or watch, a psychic can pick up energy from the object and sense the person to whom it belongs. When I handed her my car-keys on this first Reading, she held them and told me that I don't like sitting still for a minute and am a patient, methodical individual that looks for the gold in situations and usually finds it. I am not the best judge of the accuracy of her analysis. You will have to ask my friends if that describes me.

That concluded my first visit to the Other Side, which took place in March 1998. Since then I have paid more than a dozen visits. In addition to such arranged trips, if we are to believe what highly gifted Mediums like Sylvia Browne and James Van Praagh tell us, we visit the Other Side three or four times a week when we are sleeping.

Although I didn't know it at the time, my first visit turned out to be a major life change for me. This introduction to the Other Side opened up a new paranormal world that I was unaware existed. My life has not been the same since.

III.

# Give Me a Sign

My old friend Bill M, on the Other Side since May 1983, and I, agreed, before he left, that whoever passed over first would try to contact the one remaining. He was convinced that it could be done without the aid of a medium. Just as he told me on my first visit that a sign that he was around would be that I would have an itchy nose, now, this frequently happens when I am driving my car. It seems as though he is usually in the back seat helping me on my journey through my current life on earth. Beyond that we have yet to have a direct After Death Communication.

In their book "*Hello from Heaven*" Bill and Judy Guggenheim relate how they spent seven years researching the field of After Death Communication, or ADC. During that time, they collected more than 3,300 firsthand accounts from people in the United States and Canada who believe that they have been contacted by a loved one who has died. The following two ADCs are typical of the 353 accounts that they include in their book:

*Brenda works for a social service agency in Virginia. Her husband, Russell, was 42 years old when he died of a heart attack. They had always said whoever went first would find a way to communicate back to the other. And he did! About a month after Russell died, she was sitting at her desk at work when she suddenly had a strong aroma of roses! It was as strong as if there was a bouquet of roses on her desk. She knew it was from Russell! Looking around there were no roses anywhere. Nobody else smelled them. Russell used to delight in sending her roses on special occasions and sometimes 'just because.' Brenda knew he had sent them again as his way of communicating his love for her.*

*Johanna is an elementary school teacher in Massachusetts. Her daughter, Margaret, was killed in an automobile accident at age 20. Eight years later, with her husband, she planned to go to New York City for Easter weekend. Easter Sunday was a pleasant day, and so they walked to St. Patrick's Cathedral from their hotel. When they arrived they asked a policeman if they needed tickets to attend. They were quite dismayed when he told them, "There's no way you're going to get into this Mass without them!" Within a minute or so, a man stepped forward from the crowd and said, "Take my tickets," and he handed her an envelope. As readily as he appeared, he just seemed to disappear.*

*When they were escorted down the aisle to their assigned seats they found that directly, close by, was St. Margaret's altar! Johanna was joyfully overwhelmed that their daughter Margaret had sent them an exceptionally strong message, on Easter, saying, "There is a life after death, there is a heaven, and I will see you again."*

In "*Talking to Heaven,*" James Van Praagh tells us about the ways that spirits let their loved ones know that they are around them, without the use of a medium. Spirits can affect electricity in a variety of ways involving lights, TV, radios, music, clocks, phones, answering machines, appliances and computers.

"A very common sign, immediately after, or within several months following a transition, is scent. Suddenly, one becomes aware of a faint smell of a cigar, or roses, a familiar perfume or shaving lotion. These scents are definitely associated with those who have departed. For instance, a person's father might have used a particular after-shave lotion, and unexpectedly it pervades the room. These scents and odors are ways loved ones let us know that they are nearby.

Shortly after I decided to start writing my book, I dropped into Staples to pick up a cartridge for my Canon printer. The salesman was quite helpful; he suggested that I take the Staples equivalent product. I was pleasantly surprised when I arrived at the checkout counter, to be given 1,000 pages of computer paper as part of a sales promotion program to encourage the sale of Staples printer cartridges. I took that to be a sign from the Other Side that I was on the right track.

When I left the store with the paper under my arm and walked towards my car, another car pulled up beside me, and in the car was a blond Cocker Spaniel like "Buddy" with his head out the window. The last time I talked to White Fox he said that he was fond of Buddy and was patting him as we communicated. Synchronicity perhaps? I like to think that these experiences were confirmation that I should write this book. The combination of the unexpected free computer paper and Buddy's double appearing certainly seemed like an encouraging message from my Spirit Guide, White Fox.

IV.

# Guardian Angels and Spirit Guides

It was during a telephone Reading in July 2000 that I learned the names of my new Spirit Guide, White Fox, and my Guardian Angel, Chlora. While each of us has a Guardian Angel and one or more Spirit Guides, I have been blessed with mine.

White Fox, my Spirit Guide, loves horses, and the outdoors with water. He has had many lives here, including one as a judge. Described as having flowing white hair and crystal blue eyes he loves my dog Buddy who is there with him. He tells me that he is 'waiting for me to share my message with the world.' Your Spirit Guides will inspire, recommend and stand behind you as you work toward the goals you have set for your current life before you were born. Tempted as they might be, they will not deprive us of our free will, although at times I think White Fox is pushing it a little. He is quite anxious to have me write this book.

Your Spirit Guide is often with you throughout your life. Normally you work with him/her, on the Other Side, to decide the goals and objectives you wish to achieve before you leave for another lifetime here on earth. He or she will watch over you and help you until you return. However, it seems, that in my case it was a little different. In my July 2000 Reading I was told that White Fox was my *new* Spirit Guide. Since then, I have been getting strong hints about writing a book.

My Guardian Angel Chlora, was described as a beautiful Angel who provides healing, health and pure love. She likes numbers, adores bells, chimes and sunshine as well as the colors yellow and orange.

Unlike Spirit Guides, Angels have never lived on Earth. Sylvia Browne in her book *"Life on the Other Side"* tells us "Angels never speak, even to each other. Their communication is exclusively telepathic. They keep to themselves, exuding their powerful love wherever they go. Whether they're protecting us from harm, saving lives, or simply bringing us messages of joy, hope, comfort, and love, Angels are truly God's mightiest, most direct link between here and the Other Side." Telepathy is communication between minds by means other than the normal sensory channels.

During another Reading which took place soon after I finally decided to proceed with my book, Beulah, a Specialized Helper, arrived. Specialized Helpers are spirits who are attracted to us based on certain activities or work in which we are engaged. These guides possess a certain expertise in a field we are endeavoring to undertake. Usually, these beings are experts in their particular fields of knowledge. For instance, if you decide to write a mystery story, your thoughts will draw a spirit to you who have worked on, or have specialized in that particular type of writing. Beulah, a flamboyant actress from the 1920s, not unlike Tallulah Bankhead, is very animated, with a dramatic air of confidence, wears a beautiful dress and holds a long cigarette holder. She tells me that she is interested in my book, and suggested that I try running ideas by her.

V.

# Starting Over Again

On 13 May 2003, around 3:00 am, I awoke to find two strangers in my bedroom. A couple of dedicated paramedics were about to strap me to a stretcher. My family had alerted them when, alarmed by my abnormal breathing, they couldn't wake me. I just wanted to roll over and go back to sleep. After some protesting, I remember reluctantly agreeing to go to the hospital for a checkup. The 911 call made by my family had resulted in the arrival of two police cars, a firetruck and an ambulance on my normally quiet residential street. I must have lost consciousness again, for the next thing I remember was lying in the ambulance parked in front of my home and uncertain about where I was, struggling to get free. I was drifting in and out of consciousness, in the ambulance, on the way to the hospital.

At the emergency ward, I was given a comprehensive series of tests to try and determine the cause of my apparent seizure. I was surprised when the diagnosis was epilepsy, because it usually affects younger patients and no one in my family has it.

In a Reading later that month, Jan Remington, a clairvoyant and Medium told me that it was during this seizure that I decided to start another life. She told me that when we prepare a life chart before we leave the Other Side, we build in several possible escape routes, called exit points, where we can decide to return to the Other Side, when we feel that we have accomplished what we intended to do when we came here. Apparently I felt I had more to achieve, including writing this book. Which leads me to believe that during my apparent seizure I was over on the Other Side meeting with my Spirit Guides and Angels preparing a new life chart that covered what I would try to accomplish in my extended lifetime. Sometimes when people are releasing a lot of old negative energy from their bodies, it almost looks like a seizure. The body moves and vibrates in a very similar fashion. My friend Angelika, feels that this might be the case for me since my body had to release things to bring me to a healthy immunity and a lighter place to live longer.

My medium, Jan, tells me that when I had my apparent seizure, I not only decided to start an extended lifetime in this body, but three members of the Group of Eight Infinite Divine Light also came into my life. One was Archangel Rafael, the Angel of Healing who helps me to help others by sending unconditional love to handicapped people. Another was Eagle Starfire, a Blackfoot medicine man who speaks for many, who told me that it is important to honor his heritage, and that he would like his message told in the old way, as in a story passed on by the elders. The third member is Isis, an Egyptian Goddess, who, by the period of the Roman Empire, had become the most prominent deity of the Mediterranean basin. These travelers in the 5th dimension protect me, and help me send unconditional love to handicapped people. Each day as I say my morning prayers, I invite them into my life that they may help me to help others. Throughout the day, I call on them to help me extend a Shambhalan prayer field that sends unconditional love to those I see around me who are handicapped. I agree with the Dalai Lama that: *"Our prime purpose in life is to help others. And if you can't help them, at least don't hurt them."*

VI.

# Using The Secret of Shambhala

In the Tibetan Buddhist tradition, Shambhala is a mystical kingdom hidden somewhere beyond the snow peaks of the Himalayas. It is mentioned in various ancient texts, including the Kalachakra Tantra and the ancient texts of the Zhang Zhung culture which pre-dated Tibetan Buddhism in western Tibet.

The Dalai Lama has said the following, with regard to Shambhala:

*"Although those with special affiliation may actually be able to go there through their karmic connection, nevertheless it is not a physical place that we can actually find. We can only say that it is a pure land in the human realm. And unless one has the merit and the actual karmic association one cannot actually arrive there."*

During my third Reading with Jan Remington, in July 2000, I was told that a book *"The Secret of Shambhala"* would give me a hint regarding an upcoming project. At the time, I had not read the book, nor was I aware of an upcoming project to which it might apply. In Tibetan, Shambhala means "the source of happiness", and in his inspirational novel, *"The Secret of Shambhala"*, James Redfield features a mythical community located in the mountains near Tibet, called

Shambhala, where there is knowledge that has been kept hidden for hundreds of years, and is the source of an insight that can have a profound impact on our lives. The people of Shambhala believe that inside you is a great power that can be extended, a mental energy called prayer and that you must learn that you have a prayer-energy-field flowing out from you at all times.

Also, in Tibetan, Rten brel means synchronicity. And the people of Shambhala believe that you must set your field to stay in the synchronistic process, to bring the intuitions and the coincidences to help you. Setting a field for synchronicity is a matter of putting yourself in a particular state of mind. One must visualize that one's energy is going out and bringing just the right hunches and the right events to you. You have to expect them to occur at any moment.

Redfield tells us "the Shambhalan people embrace the concept that our prayer-field flows out in front of us and that we can set it to uplift anyone around us. When your prayer field reaches other people in this way, they feel a hit of spiritual energy. Therefore you should endeavor to learn the steps that extend the human prayer-field to connect with divine energy and let it flow through with love."

In 1976, Trungpa Rinpoche began giving teachings, (since gathered and presented as Shambhala Training), inspired by his vision of the legendary Kingdom of Shambhala. Shambhalian practices focus on using mindfulness/awareness meditation as a means of connecting with one's basic sanity and using that insight as inspiration for one's encounter with the world. Shambhala Training is essentially a secular approach to meditation rooted in Buddhism but accessible to individuals of any, or no, religion.

The Shambhala and Buddhist teachings can be studied and explored in the worldwide association of meditation centers. These centers were originally founded by Vidyadhara the Venerable Chögyam Trungpa Rinpoche and now directed by his son and spiritual heir, Sakyong Mipham Rinpoche, from the Shambhala International Headquarters in Halifax, Nova Scotia, Canada.

The network of over 170 Shambhala Centers includes both centers in the city for regular practice and study, and also centers in the country for more intensive programs. At the web site of the organization: http://www.shambhala.org/ we are informed that instruction follows the tradition of oral transmission from teacher to student that goes back twenty-five hundred years. Meditation instruction is available free of charge at all Centers.

VII.

# How Do We Know
# What It's Like There?

That first visit to the Other Side in 1998 stimulated my curiosity. It made me wonder what it was like there. Since I have never had a NDE, I cannot speak from firsthand knowledge, however, an old Chinese Proverb tells us that to know the road ahead, ask those coming back. In other words, one of the best ways to determine the characteristics of another world is to ask someone who has been there. For example, some time ago, I traveled to Hong Kong on a business trip, and before leaving, I naturally asked a friend who had recently returned, for his impressions of the place. In much the same way, a source of information regarding the Other Side lies in the descriptions provided by those who have been there while having a Near Death Experience.

The reported experiences of those persons who have returned after being declared clinically dead have confirmed my belief that there is indeed life after death that is lived in an incredibly beautiful heavenly home. One definition of an NDE is: "a phenomenon in which a person clinically dies or comes very close to death only to be revived, and then can recall in great detail, descriptions of spiritual worlds and other supernatural events."

One of the standard texts on NDE experiences is "Life After Life", a book by Dr. Raymond A. Moody, which offers true experiences of those people declared clinically "dead." The Near Death Experience Research Foundation (www. nderf.org) reports that 774 NDEs occur each day in the United States. This means that about one person in twenty has had an NDE. Often people that have had such an experience are reluctant to talk about it, because when they do, disbelieving family and friends often express extreme skepticism and are derisive and scornful.

The critics of NDEs come mostly from that group of people who believe in a mechanical world. Those who believe nothing exists beyond the physical. This includes scientists who have theorized that NDEs can be induced by chemical, electrical, and/or severe loss of oxygen to the brain. A few of these scientists have run experiments with drugs and announced that they induced NDEs in their subjects. While it is true, that the subjects of these experiments, did experience a few of the background events common to most NDEs, such as seeing light, feeling loved, knowledge of oneness, etc., none of the subjects experienced an authentic NDE. What they did experience is common to what meditation experts experience without drugs. Drugs do not cause the experience; they only allow it to happen by lowering the physical perception and focus. Unfortunately the media gives credit to what they say and as a result many people have become misinformed. This misinformation will continue to proliferate until the public learns more truth about the NDE phenomenon. No one using any drug or artificial stimulus has induced a NDE in anyone.

For an incredible account of one woman's near death experience see the book, "Embraced by the Light" by Betty Eadie. One reviewer, Kimberly Clark-Sharp, the President of the Seattle International Association of Near Death

Experiences was quoted as saying: "Even after interviewing over one thousand near death experiencers, Betty Eadie's account remains the most detailed and spellbinding near death experience I have heard. What happened to Betty is thought-provoking, inspirational and comforting."

Psychic medium, John Edwards, in his book "One Last Time" tells us that sometimes mediums are accused of being "just mind readers" that pick up brain waves from their clients and say they are from the spirits of the dead. After all, the subconscious mind is where the total body of knowledge of all our previous lives resides. As a medium, he frequently has to prove, to confirmed cynics, that he is legitimate.

Since I have never had a Near Death Experience, I am not speaking from firsthand knowledge when I describe what it is like on the Other Side. However, the reported experiences of those persons who have returned after being declared clinically dead, have confirmed my belief that there is indeed life after death that is lived in an incredible heavenly home.

Although I have never had a NDE, I know someone who has. My Mystic friend, Rene Beaupre, has made two visits via NDE, both as a result of lightning strikes. Rene calls himself a Mystic because of his training in various forms of divination as well as earthly religions and metaphysics.

We are told by those who have been there while having a Near Death Experience, that when you enter the World on the Other Side, you will find that it is not 'up there' somewhere above the clouds, but that your heavenly home exists all around you in another dimension, operating on a higher frequency than our own, and only three feet above our ground level here on Earth.

When you arrive there, your first impression will be one of unbelievable loveliness, in an impeccable world of green fields, and majestic forests. In the midst of this elegance are amazing buildings, made of shimmering crystal-like materials not seen on earth. Buildings are perfect there; every line and angle and detail is created to perfectly complement the entire structure. Inside these prodigious structures, all types of schools, libraries and research centers are located. On the Other Side, courses on every imaginable subject are available. Work and study continue nonstop on medical, scientific and psychological progress for the benefit of Earth.

In one of her many informative books, *"Life on the Other Side,"* Sylvia Browne gives us a comprehensive description of what it's like to live there. In the chapter dealing with 'Careers, Research and Recreation' she tells us:

*"Believe it or not, one of our greatest sources of fun is studying. There's no doubt about it, we are much smarter on the Other Side than we are here. Our minds broaden again to their full potential when we get there. Memories of all our past lives and everything we learned during them come flooding back in an exhilarating rush, unblocked from the cluttered chaotic boundaries of earthly consciousness."*

There is no such thing as "time" in this spiritual world, no past, present and future. Everything is "now." As an amateur clocksmith who enjoys restoring antique clocks, I find it hard to get used to the idea that there are no clocks or watches there. Existing without minutes, hours and days seems nearly impossible to us modern earthbound creatures. But there really is no such thing as time in the context of eternity on the Other Side. A nice long lifetime on earth is perceived by the spirits on the Other Side as a quick trip away from Home. Time is accelerated and days on Earth may be only minutes for souls.

Advanced Psychics like Sylvia Browne and James Van Praagh tell us that on the Other Side, the sun, moon and stars are not visible. Day and night do not exist there. The light is a consistent combination of exquisite, subdued colors.

Regardless of what age we are when we die, when we cross over we become thirty years of age. We do not keep any injuries, or handicaps from our recent lifetime.

Sex, as we know it in our earthly life, does not exist there. Instead, another quite superior form of affection called "merging" is practiced. Two souls can merge and unite together on a physical, spiritual, and emotional level that results in requited ecstasy.

At my age, I hate having to get up frequently in the middle of the night, to relieve myself. When I finally return Home, again, this will no longer bother me, because there is no need for bathrooms there, nor night for that matter. Most of the animals we loved here on earth are alive and well on the Other Side. For example, my Cocker Spaniel "Buddy" is waiting there for me to come Home.

VIII.

# Help from the Other Side

In September 1999, following a suggestion from my friend Bill, I began the Course in Miracles. In the Workbook for *A Course in Miracles* (ACIM), which is a 365-day set of psychological exercises, we are given a very specific curriculum for relinquishing a thought system based on fear and accepting instead a thought system based on love. Each day we are given a specific thought to focus on, eyes closed, for a specific amount of time. At the beginning of each day, for a year as I took the course on my own I kept a record of my progress, in a journal. Although I didn't always understand what some of the lessons meant I accepted them on faith. As I worked my way through the course I had the feeling that I was ready for a life style change.

"*A Course In Miracles*" published by The Foundation for Inner Peace teaches that love is a miracle which surpasses all others, and that all other true miracles are in fact intended to bring people to the awareness of love itself. I found that taking the ACIM course gave me a gradual shift in perception; it changed my perspective so that I now look at those around me differently. I try to be kind to others because I believe that *everyone you meet is doing the best they can, while fighting a hard battle.* We are each on a journey that began and will end on the Other Side. I find that I am now particularly concerned about those who are disabled or handicapped.

Sometimes we think we are using our ingenuity when we come up with a 'brainwave' or we might say, "an idea came to me." However the brainwave, or idea, may not have been ours to begin with, but rather it may have been a gift from the spirit world. Our Spirit Guides can contact us in a number of ways. One of the most common is by telepathy. This is communication directly from one mind to another without speech or writing. We are particularly receptive to telepathy from the Other Side just after we wake up. First thing in the morning I try to sit quietly with an open mind to provide my Spirit Guides an opportunity to contact me. I am convinced that I am receiving help with this book from my friends beyond the veil. White Fox, my Spirit Guide, advises me to "relax and let it flow through." On one visit to the Other Side, Beulah, my Specialized Helper, told me she was interested in my book. She was familiar with what I had covered and suggested changes that were quite helpful. For example, she told me that my description of Archangel Rafael was satisfactory but I needed to do more work on Eagle Star Fire.

Larry Dossey, M.D., at the beginning of his remarkable book *"Reinventing Medicine"* states;

*"The premise of this book is that the mind is infinite. This means that my mind touches, and is touched by, those of everyone else, and that all minds are linked together. This creates challenges in acknowledging the sources of one's ideas, because their possible origins include everyone who has a mind."*

Johann Wolfgang von Goethe, German poet, and natural philosopher wrote:

*"Everyone of my writings has been furnished to me by a thousand different persons, a thousand different things".*

I have received several additional reminders that "I am not alone." In a visit to the Other Side I made during August 2003, Alf M., my deceased brother-in-law, was there, waiting to tell me that 'I have a platoon of people helping me.' White Fox also mentioned earlier that 'I have a houseful of Spirit Guides that are anxious to help.' There are several precedents that support this sort of thing happening, and the writers of "A Course in Miracles", and "Conversations With God", were convinced that their books were dictated from the Other Side.

"A Course in Miracles" began with the sudden decision of two people to join in a common goal. Their names were Helen Schucman and William Thetford, Professors of Medical Psychology at Columbia University's College of Physicians and Surgeons in New York City. Ms Schucman explains her involvement, as follows:

*"Three startling months preceded the actual writing, during which time Bill suggested that I write down the highly symbolic dreams and descriptions of the strange images that were coming to me. Although I had grown more accustomed to the unexpected by that time, I was still very surprised when I wrote, "This is a course in miracles." That was my introduction to the Voice. It made no sound, but seemed to be giving me a kind of rapid, inner dictation, which I took down in a shorthand notebook. I would take down what the Voice "said" and read it back to Bill the next day and he typed it from my dictation. The whole process took about seven years."*

In *"Conversations with God"* Neale Donald Walsch, in the uncommon dialogue revealed in his books is convinced that he did not write them. In Book 1, he writes:

*"Before I knew it, I had begun a conversation and I was not writing as much as taking dictation. The process is simple. I put pen to paper, ask a question, and see what thoughts come to mind.*

*If no words are given to me, I put everything away for another day."*

Wayne Dyer also recollects that when he was writing his book *"Inspiration: Your Ultimate Calling"* he awoke every morning at around 3:30, and sat down to write. He would place his hand on the table and allow the ideas to flow from the world of Spirit through his heart and onto the page. He feels that he is merely an instrument through which ideas are expressed.

The spirits on the Other Side are constantly active, studying, researching working on cures for earthly diseases to transmit to our doctors and scientists telepathically so they can "discover" them.

Advanced Psychic Mediums like Sylvia Browne tell us that a medical breakthrough, like the recent announcement that researchers in both Wisconsin and Japan have managed to create human embryonic stem cells, might well have originated on the Other Side. Sylvia says that information is frequently given to two different research groups, here on earth, at the same time.

# IX

# A Family Reunion

Our journeys through life begin and end on the Other Side. Before we leave to start a new life we decide, with help from our Spirit Guides, what we want to learn from our next life that will make us a better person. These decisions include choosing our parents and where we would like to live.

My current journey through this life on Earth started in the small railway town of Lindsay, located 76 miles east of Toronto, on the 25th day of June 1923. It all began around noon; I was born on the kitchen table, in my maternal grand-parent's home. As the first male grandchild, and the first of three children my parents Percy and Bernice would have, I was spoiled. But then I spoil so easily. My grandfather Heber was a barber who liked to go fishing for trout on Sunday mornings. Grandmother Annie Williamson was noted for her homemade quilts and apple pies.

My Mother was active in the Ladies Aid, and whenever there was a Church supper she could always be found in the kitchen perspiring profusely while helping prepare the meal. She was a small town girl with a kind and generous heart. For example, one day during the Depression, we were expecting delivery of ten bags of coal for our furnace. When they arrived she asked the deliveryman to drop off two of the bags at neighbors down the street, who couldn't afford to buy coal. Needless to say when Dad came home and noticed the loss he was not pleased. In those days, most homes were heated with coal-fired furnaces, and these were notoriously difficult to operate effectively. Ask anyone more than 65-years-old, who grew up in Canada, what they remember about tending the fire in the coal furnace. Most of them will shudder, shake their head, wince and reply, "Those things were awful." A wood or coal furnace has a sealed firebox where the fuel is burned, and a heat exchanger where air is warmed before delivery upstairs. We were lucky in that my father, relying on his work experience, could bank a coal fire to make it last right through the night. Less experienced neighbors would wake in the morning to a very cold house.

Although my Dad didn't attend church he was none-the-less, a God-fearing railway fireman who before the advent of automatic stokers would sometimes shovel eight tons of coal in a day. Dad grew up in Westerham Hill, Kent south of London, England. He and his three brothers helped their father, William grow strawberries for sale at London's Covent Garden Fruit and Vegetable Market. During the First World War, as a member of the Canadian Infantry Corps, he was badly wounded in the Battle of Vimy Ridge. I can still look back and remember how, although it was many years after the War, he would often sleep with the bedclothes pulled up over his head. Long after the war he no longer needed to protect himself from rats—it was an automatic behavior picked up in the trenches.

One of my Readings with Jan, held in July 1999, was conducted, by telephone from her home at the time north of Toronto. When she was here on earth, my Mom suffered from a blood clot in her right foot and at this Reading Jan said she was seeing a lady with a right foot problem who said she would be looking after me for the next five months. Through Jan, Mom also told me that my father Percy was in the background—as usual. Jan asked me if one of my Grandfathers had a beard, and had plants that were not flowers. That was obviously Grandpa Westbrook, the Kentish market gardener. Jan also identified my other grandparent Heber, as the one that was with me with strings. He, and grandmother, Annie, would often take me, as a precocious four year old, for rides in the back seat of his Canadian-made McLaughlin Buick, while I serenaded them by strumming on my ukulele and singing the cowboy song "*Can I Sleep in Your Barn Tonight Mister*?" I can still remember how pleased I felt to be the center of attention, during those rides.

During this same Reading I was also told that in the next month I would be visiting a person in bed, and that he would have a loving Spirit behind a table in his room. I was told that he needed to be reassured that his mother was watching over him. At that time, my 97-year-old Uncle Perry was recovering from a minor heart attack, and I was able to tell him when I saw him later in the Oakville Trafalgar Hospital, that his mother was there with him. He was obviously pleased.

At the conclusion of this Reading I thanked Jan, and as I hung up the phone I had a warm feeling of satisfaction: knowing that members of my family were waiting there for me to join them one day, there in my home, back on the Other Side.

X.

# Judging Others

There I was one day recently, sitting off to one side enjoying a butter tart and decaf coffee, in the cafeteria of a large modern hospital, looking around me at all the people having their lunch. A few, like me, were alone, but most were in groups of like-minded friends, engaged in animated discussion that was frequently punctuated by hearty laughter. As I sat there, I couldn't help but think that they were all on a journey that started before they were born, and will end when they pass over again to the Other Side. On their individual journeys, while following a roadmap on their DNA, each one was doing the best they can with what they have.

As mentioned earlier, I found that taking the ACIM course gave me a gradual shift in perception that changed my perspective so that I look at those around me differently.

I now try to be kind to others because I believe that everyone you meet is doing the best they can while fighting a hard battle.

In her first book, *"A Return to Love,"* that sold a million copies, Marianne Williamson explains some of the principles of A Course in Miracles as they relate to issues in daily life. Williamson reveals how we can each become a miracle worker by accepting God and by the expression of love in our daily lives. Whether psychic pain is in the area of relationships, career, or health, she shows us how love is a potent force, the key to inner peace, and how, by practicing love, we can make our own lives more fulfilling while creating a more peaceful and loving world for our children.

In "*How to Know God*" Deepak Chopra presents a ground rule for looking at those around you. "The cheapest way to feel good about yourself is by feeling superior to others. From this dark seed grows every manner of judgment. Getting out of judgment is vital, and to plant that seed, you have to stop dividing others into categories of good and bad. Everyone lives in the same light. A simple formula may help here. When you are tempted to judge another person, no matter how obviously they deserve it, remind yourself that everyone is doing the best they can from his own level of consciousness."

At Christmas, I received, as a gift, a small desk calendar which, each day, provides a new "*Insight From the Dalai Lama.*" His message for 6 November 2006 was:

"*The essence of all spiritual life is your emotion, your attitude toward others. Once you have pure and sincere motivation, all the rest follows. You can develop this right attitude toward others on the basis of kindness, love and respect, and on the clear realization of the oneness of all human beings.*"

Again on the 12th of November, his message offered this:

"*All of the different religious faiths, despite their philosophical differences, have a similar objective. Every religion emphasizes human improvement, love, respect for others, sharing other people's suffering. On these lines every religion has more or less the same viewpoint and the same goal.*"

Before you can love others, you must first learn to love yourself. In this society, we're taught that praising ourselves is selfish and wrong. But praising ourselves for things that are good about ourselves only helps us. It is a healing thing to do, something that nourishes our self-worth and self-esteem. When we love ourselves, we're happier and more true to our own selves... and that happiness and ability to be free spreads to others. We all are here to learn to *love*. One of the first lessons we are trying to learn is a love of ourselves. Once we have achieved such unconditional love of self and others we become enlightened and can then live in nonjudgmental harmony with our fellow human beings.

Do you ask yourself, "How can I forgive myself for hurting others and being manipulative?" Spiritual counselor Gary Zukav explains that forgiveness is something you decide to do for yourself. When you don't Forgive... it's like wearing dark sunglasses that distort everything you see. You also want everyone else to see through these glasses. Forgiveness is taking those glasses off. Not forgiving is like carrying heavy suitcases full of books through an airport. Forgiving is putting the suitcases down and walking away without them. It is lightening up. It is being able to enjoy your life, laugh again, and see the beauty in others. When you cannot forgive yourself, you cannot forgive others. When you cannot forgive others, you cannot forgive yourself. The dynamic of forgiveness is the same in both cases.

A compassionate society is one that provides comfort where it is needed. That's a variation on the advice Bob Dylan says he got, many years ago, from his grandmother: *"Be kind, because everyone you'll ever meet is fighting a hard battle."* When we choose not to remember that, we fail our community. We fail people who need us. And we fail ourselves."

XI.

# The Power of Prayer

When I say my daily prayers, I sit hands on knees, with my palms up. By the time I say 'amen' my hands are noticeably warm from what seems to be spiritual energy. I think that this is a case of 'what goes around comes around,' when you pray for someone you direct spiritual energy to them that comes back to benefit you. When Father Sean O'Laoire, a Catholic priest and psychologist in the San Francisco Bay area conducted research on intercessory prayer, he discovered that the agents doing the praying improved more than the subjects for whom they were praying.

Deepak Chopra in *"Life After Death"* tells us that:

*"By now the public is well aware that research on prayer has validated that it works. In a typical experiment volunteers, usually from church groups, are asked to pray for sick people in the hospital. They do not visit the person and often have only a number rather than a name to go by. The prayer isn't specific; they are asked simply to pray for God's help. The results of such experiments have been startlingly positive. In the best known one, conducted at Duke University in North Carolina, patients who were prayed for recovered faster and with fewer side effects than*

*those not prayed for. Here we have one more demonstration that we are all connected by the same field of consciousness."*

In *"The Secret of Shambhala,"* James Redfield tells us that the people of Shambhala believe that inside you is a great power that can be extended, a mental energy called prayer and that you must learn that you have a prayer-energy-field flowing out from you at all times.

In his compelling book, *"Reinventing Medicine,"* Larry Dossey, M.D. informs us that many scientific studies reveal that healing can be achieved at a distance by directing loving and compassionate thoughts, intentions and prayers to others who may even be unaware these efforts are being extended to them.

The Archangel of Healing, Rafael, first came into my life when my extended life began following my seizure. The psychic medium Jan told me then, that with his help, I would send unconditional love to the handicapped.

When I am out in public and see someone who is disabled or handicapped, I use the Shambhalan prayer field that allows the three members of the Group of Eight to extend, through me to the handicapped person, good health, peace of mind and unconditional love.

I was intrigued when I read about prayer on the Other Side, as described by Betty Eadie following her profound Near Death Experience in *"Embraced By The Light."*

*"The heavens scrolled back and I saw the sphere of earth rotating in space. I saw many lights shooting up from the earth like beacons. Some were very broad and charged into heaven like broad laser beams. Others resembled the illumination of small penlights, and some were mere sparks. I was surprised as I was told these beams of power were the prayers of people on earth.*

*I saw angels rushing to answer the prayers. They were organized to give as much help as possible. As they worked within this organization, they literally flew from person to person, from prayer* to prayer, and were filled with love and joy by their work. They delighted to help us and were especially joyful when somebody prayed with enough intensity and faith to be answered immediately. They always responded to the brighter, larger prayers first, and then each prayer in turn, until all of them were answered. I did notice, however that insincere prayers of repetition have little if any light; and having no power, are not heard.

I was distinctly told that all prayers of desire are heard and answered. When we have great need, or when we are praying for other people, the beams project straight from us and are immediately visible. Our prayers for others have great strength but can only be answered as far as they do not infringe on the others' free will—or as long as they do not frustrate others' needs."

My amateur radio friend Copthorne Macdonald writes in "Getting a Life":

"We must keep all negative thoughts out of our heads concerning other people. If our fear turns to anger and we lapse into thinking the worst of others, a negative prayer goes out that tends to create in them exactly the behavior we expect. That's why teachers who expect great things from their students usually get it and when they expect the negative they get that too."

In an earlier book, "Recovering the Soul," Dr. Larry Dossey, introduced the concept of "nonlocal mind" -- mind unconfined to the brain and body, mind spread infinitely throughout space and time. Since then, many leading scientists have adopted "nonlocal mind" as an emerging image of consciousness. Dr. Dossey's ever-deepening explication of nonlocal mind provides a legitimate foundation for the merging of spirit and medicine. The ramifications of such a union are radical and call for no less than the reinvention of medicine.

In 1997, at Harvard University, a conference called "Intercessory Prayer and Distant Healing Intention: Clinical and Laboratory Research" was convened. Approximately one hundred researchers from medical schools and universities in the United States were there to discuss experiments in nonlocal healing that they were performing at their institutions. They all had a common goal—to test whether or not individuals could mentally help heal distant persons who were unaware they were doing so. These were world class scholars highly respected in their fields, forthrightly discussing their findings about the power of prayer. Many of the studies the scientists presented at Harvard have since been published in professional journals.

## Praying for Patients with AIDS

One of the studies discussed at the Harvard conference dealt with one of the greatest medical challenges of today: AIDS.

Dr. Elizabeth Targ and her colleagues at California Pacific Medical Centre in San Francisco tested whether distant healing, including prayer, has a therapeutic effect on health in AIDS, when patients do not know they are receiving treatment. The controlled, randomized clinical trial used the same rigorous scientific standards that are required for testing a new drug. Forty patients with advanced AIDS—thirty-seven men and three women—were recruited through advertisements and fliers. They were from various ethnic and cultural groups. All the patients received standard medical care for their illness. Twenty however, received distance-healing intentions in addition. The study was double blind, so no one involved, including the patients and the scientists, knew who was in the distant healing group.

Forty volunteers throughout the United States and Canada conducted the distant healing therapy. Each healer was given a patient's first name and photograph to help the healer to develop a personal connection with the subject. Healers were asked to focus their mental energies on the patient's health and well-being for an hour a day, six days a week, for ten weeks. Healers were from eight different healing traditions, including Christian, Jewish, Buddhist, Native American, and shamanic practices. The healers had an average of seventeen years experience. They were organized on a rotating schedule so that a different healer treated each patient each week. A blind review of the patient's medical charts revealed several significant differences. Those patients who had received distant or non-local healing intentions had undergone significantly fewer new AIDS-related illnesses, had less severe illnesses, required fewer doctor visits, fewer hospitalizations, and fewer days of hospitalization. Moreover, those receiving distant-healing showed a significantly improved moods compared with the controls. The psychological tests showed that the treatment effects were not affected by which group the subjects believed they were in.

Data also shows that if patients undergoing cardiac surgery are prayed for, they experience 50 to100 percent fewer complications from the surgery than patients who are not prayed for, and their surgical incisions heal faster. In his book *Reinventing Medicine,* Larry Dossey describes a future hospital using nonlocal healing that would be connected to an international prayer network that includes all of the major religions. Within minutes of a patient arriving in an emergency room, prayer groups would be alerted electronically.

### In-the-Zone

As participants and spectators of sports, many of us are aware of those epiphanies in which a sporting activity or event seems to go beyond the basic play-by-play to a higher dimension or spiritual level. In these experiences, everything comes together in a flow, and the activity itself takes on a religious or mythic experience. Such nonlocal states of consciousness may include prayer, meditation, trance, and dreaming, as well as mystical, out-of-body, and near-death experiences.

Nonlocal experiences are particularly common in sports. Making a place for nonlocal mind helps athletes understand what they call "in-the-zone." Bill Russell is one of the greatest basketball players of all time. He had a very powerful experience when he was 16. A warm feeling accompanied by a sense that he was all right suddenly possessed him, a feeling of "everything is alright; his first experience of being "in-the-zone." Russell became famous for his amazing defensive moves, including blocked shots, which were not done in those days. When he was at his best during a game he was in "the zone."

Although I haven't had a sporting nonlocal experience I have had several peak experiences. American psychologist and philosopher Abraham H. Maslow (1908-1970) coined the term *peak experience*. He first spoke of *peak experiences* forty years ago. It was his terminology for a breakthrough into expanded consciousness.

Peak experiences are sudden feelings of intense happiness and well-being, and the unity of all things. Accompanying these experiences is a heightened sense of control over the body and emotions, together with a wider sense of awareness. Such experiences are not uncommon. For instance, a UK survey revealed that 56% of those surveyed said that they have had a peak experience. Peak experiences are those moments, lasting from seconds to minutes, during which we feel the highest levels of happiness, harmony and possibility. They range in degree from intensification of everyday pleasures, to apparently 'supernatural' episodes of enhanced consciousness which feel qualitatively distinct from, and superior to, normal experience. It was nearly impossible however to prove that anyone lived at a peak for any length of time. Out of the whole population, Maslow could barely find 5 percent who even temporarily made such a transition. This handful of people were labeled "self actualized."

Looking back, I have had three peak experiences The first happened some twenty years ago when I was sitting off to one side at the Ottawa Airport, waiting for my daughter to return from a business trip to Toronto. Lasting for but a few minutes, I had a wonderful, warm, confident feeling of heightened awareness that I could do anything, which is what my spirit guide, White Fox, keeps telling me. I do think, however, that we have to draw the line at brain surgery and rocket science. The PEs happened before he came into my life.

The main difference between 'the zone' and a peak experience is the time duration. While most PEs last a minute or two, athletes like the basketball player Russell, and others, can go for a much longer period when they are in "the zone."

XII.

# Reincarnation

Back in November of 2005, when my Mother told me that Dad was reborn in Ethiopia, I was surprised; not that he was back on this side again, but rather at his speedy return to another earthly life. When I first heard this news of my father's reincarnation, it left me feeling cut-off from him. Despite the fact that during my visits he had tended to remain in the background it had always been reassuring to know that he was available if I wanted to contact him. He must have been anxious to continue with the growth and learning of his soul. Recently however, I came to understand about parallel lives and soul duality from reading Michael Newton's profound *"Journey of Souls."* From this I was pleased to learn that my father's spirit could be in two places at the same time. Because of the dual capability of all souls, part of our light energy always remains behind in the spirit world. It is thus possible to make contact with a loved one, even though he may have died thirty Earth years previously and reincarnated once more.

I believe that our soul survives, after our body is dead. What happens to our body is clear. It decomposes and returns to Earth, "ashes to ashes, dust to dust." Nevertheless the reality of a human is not his body, but his or her soul. The phrase 'ashes to ashes, dust to dust' cannot be found in the Bible. It comes from the funeral service in the Book of Common Prayer.

In Latin, reincarnation means "in flesh again." We cycle through our lifetimes just as nature cycles through the seasons. If you believe in reincarnation, you are in good company. I agree with the eighteenth century French philosopher, Voltaire, when he said "It is not more surprising to be born twice than once; everything in nature is resurrection." I inherited a love of growing roses from my father. In my garden, my favorite rose "Chicago Peace" comes back again, each year, in spite of our severe Canadian winters. Each spring, I marvel at the changes that occur in my garden. It seems as though, in only a few weeks time, the trees, that were bare, are soon bursting with beautiful new growth.

Long before Voltaire, fifth-century Athenian, Socrates, who set the standard for subsequent Western philosophy, stated:

*"I am confident that there truly is such a thing as living again, that the living spring from the dead, and that the souls of the dead are in existence."*

In such beliefs, a new personality is developed during each life in the physical world, based upon past integrated experience and new acquired experiences, but some part of the being remains constantly present throughout these successive lives as well. This doctrine is a central tenet within the majority of Hindu traditions such as Yoga, Vaishnavism, Jainism and Sikhism. Although the concept of Rebirth is also a major part of Buddhist philosophy, this often differs somewhat from the Vedic based viewpoints of the Hindu traditions in defining what it is that is actually born again. From this we can see that belief in reincarnation is an ancient phenomenon. In various guises humans have believed in a future life since the ancient Egyptians, perhaps earlier, and ancient graves containing both people and possessions appear to testify to beliefs that a person would have need for their treasured possessions once again despite physical death.

## HINDUISM

In India, the idea of reincarnation is first introduced in the Upanishads (c. 800 BCE ), which are philosophical and religious texts composed in Sanskrit. The doctrine of reincarnation is absent in the Vedas, which are considered by historians to be the oldest of the Hindu scriptures.

The idea that the soul of any living being (including animals, humans and plants) reincarnates, is intricately linked to karma, another concept first introduced in the Upanishads. Karma (literally: action) is the sum of one's actions, and is the force that determines one's next reincarnation.

The cycle of death and rebirth, governed by karma, is referred to as samsara. The ideas of reincarnation, karma, and samsara are found both in Hinduism, Buddhism, Jainism and Sikhism. In all these religious traditions, ultimate salvation is liberation, moksha or mukti from the cycle of death and rebirth. In Buddhism, this liberation is often referred to as nirvana. Other Bhakti traditions regard liberation from samsara as the beginning of true spiritual life, which continues beyond nirvana freed from the worldly nature.

## BUDDHISM

Since according to Buddhism there is no permanent and unchanging soul there can be no metempsychosis in the strict sense. However, the Buddha himself referred to his past-lives. It can be inferred that these existed only in the world of the mind and that this is furthermore exactly the same state as is perceived by the one experiencing (or immersed in) the cyclic manifestation of Samsara. Buddhism never rejected Samsara, the process of rebirth or reincarnation; there is debate, however, over what is transmitted between lives.

In spite of the doctrinal beliefs against the idea of a soul, Tibetan Buddhists do believe that a new-born child may be the reincarnation of someone departed. In Tibetan Buddhism the soul of an important lama (like the Dalai Lama) is supposed to pass into an infant born nine months after his decease.

### GREEK PHILOSOPHY

Some ancient Greek philosophers believed in reincarnation; see for example Plato's Phaedo and The Republic. Pythagoras was probably the first Greek philosopher to advance the idea. The earliest Greek thinker with whom metempsychosis is connected is Pherecydes; but Pythagoras, who is said to have been his pupil, is its first famous philosophic exponent. Pythagoras probably neither invented the doctrine nor imported it from Egypt, but made his reputation by bringing Orphic doctrine from North-Eastern Hellas to Magna Graecia and by instituting societies for its diffusion.

### JUDAISM AND KABBALAH

The notion of reincarnation is not openly mentioned in the Hebrew Bible. The classical rabbinic works (midrash, Mishna and Talmud) also are silent on this topic.

While ancient Greek philosophers like Plato and Socrates attempted to prove the existence of reincarnation through philosophical proofs, Jewish mystics who accepted this idea did not. Rather, they offered explanations of why reincarnation would solve otherwise intractable problems of theodicy (how to reconcile the existence of evil with the premise of a good God.)

## CHRISTIANITY

A 2001 Gallup poll reveals that only 25 % of Americans believe in reincarnation. Almost all present official Christian denominations reject reincarnation. Exceptions include the Liberal Catholic Church and the Rosicrucian Fellowship. Reincarnation was written of in the New Testament until the time of Constantine, when the Romans censored it. There are several passages that some people claim demonstrate that a belief in reincarnation was prevalent amongst those of Jesus' inner circle. For example, in John 1:21 Jesus is asked if he is Elias and in Matthew 16:13-14 Jesus asks his disciples, 'Who do men say that I, the Son of Man, am?' And they said, 'Some say that you are John the Baptist; some, Elias; and others, Jeremias, or one of the other prophets.' Such statements are only comprehensible if Jesus' disciples believed in reincarnation.

XIII.

# Testing Beulah

Early in 2005, while writing my book, I was experiencing difficulty trying to decide how best to deal with
my description of the three members of the Group of Eight
Infinite Divine Light that are helping me each day to help
others that are handicapped. During an earlier Reading,
Beulah, my Specialized Helper, while offering to help with
my book, had suggested that I 'try her', and it occurred to me
that this might be a good test. Consequently I decided to do a
web search to see if I could come up with a Medium, closer to
Ottawa, who I could more conveniently use to help me contact people on the Other Side. Of the several local Mediums
that I found with the help of Google, Wendy James looked to
be the most suitable. Located about 25 miles away on a farm
near Metcalfe, her web site at: www.luvdragons.com mentioned that she would be attending an upcoming Psychic Fair.
When I contacted her by telephone, she readily answered
all of my questions, and although Wendy considers herself
a Psychic, she proved to be a competent Medium, as well.
Keeping my 9:00 am appointment with her at the Psychic
Fair, I found Wendy to be a down-to-earth, personable, and
friendly young woman. In addition to wanting to take Beulah

up on her offer to help with my book, I had a list of those on the Other Side I hoped to contact. At the beginning of this Reading, Wendy told me that a beautiful slender woman, who I assume was Beulah, had approached her at home, earlier in the day, and said she was anxious to contact me. Sure enough, she was there when we crossed over. When I explained to her what I was trying to do, Beulah told me that Archangel Rafael was already adequately described, and suggested that we carry on to consider Eagle StarFire.

Eagle StarFire told us that it was important to honor the heritage of his people. He told me not to exaggerate information, and to be sure and stick with tradition. In his tribe, traditional messages are told like a story accompanied by drumming. He noted that although I have no native heritage in my blood, he would like me to expose myself to his style of story telling. On my next visit to the Other Side, I will try to contact Isis, the third member of the Group of Eight.

My Spirit Guide, White Fox, was there. Described by Wendy as having the beautiful face of an angel, with white hair and crystal blue eyes, he told me he has been working with me for six years and not to worry about this book, because it will all fall into place. I should not feel rushed. "All my guides will be with me. I am going to have a house full. I am currently taking it out of the research stage and putting it in physical form. Information flows abundantly through me. I am to work on the format." He said that; "I am on the crest of the hill and it will get easier soon."

Bill M. was first on my list of loved ones who have passed over that I wished to contact. He was right there, telling Wendy that he was happy to hear from me. She asked if we had some sort of agreement over which one of us would outlast the other because he said I won. When I asked him if he was going to help me with my book he told Wendy that he will try to do whatever I would like, although he is still trying to learn how to maneuver over there, figuring out how to move around. He said that he couldn't guarantee that he will be able to get me the information I need, but he will do the best he can. Bill told Wendy that he hears me every time I speak to him, but unfortunately I do not hear him when he replies. He said we don't need a medium, and he told Wendy in a nice way that she could move aside, because we don't need her. He feels that I am trying too hard to hear him and it's not really that difficult. He also mentioned that he sits beside me while I drink a bitter drink, and as near as I can figure, he was referring to the instant decaf coffee that I have with my breakfast. At that point, Bill showed Wendy a new driveway that made her wonder what it meant, until I pointed out that I had recently had mine rebuilt.

On this visit, I was particularly hoping to see if I could contact my American amateur radio friend, Bill DeW, who had recently passed over. Formerly, Bill and I would enjoy daily early morning radio conversations. He lived in Rochester, N.Y., and always had the best of equipment that ensured a strong signal into Canada. Following his retirement from Kodak, he had enjoyed playing strenuous games of tennis until his knees gave out on him and confined him to a wheelchair. I wanted to ask him if he was playing tennis again. When we contacted him, Bill told Wendy that although he no longer plays, he enjoys visiting all the best courts in England and going out on them, when nobody's there. He told me he regrets not finishing his writing when he was here, and he wants me to finish mine.

Sometimes, a troubled spirit does not want to leave the Earth following death. This is usually the result of an unresolved situation that has an impact on its consciousness. In effect they are dead, but for personal reasons, they won't go Home. For example, when I checked in with Stu G., another of my deceased amateur radio friends, he said he was worried about our friend Jim J. When Stu passed over a year earlier, Jim, who was already there, had taken Stu under his wing and helped him make the transition to the Other Side. However, Stu felt that Jim was now very earthbound. His wife Elizabeth had recently had a bad fall in which she broke her hip, and with his wife in hospital, Jim wanted to stay close to her. As Stu put it, he felt 'that old bugger is not taking care of himself.' In these unusual cases, help is available from higher caring entities from the Other Side that can assist in the adjustment process.

XIV.

# Killed for Writing

I admire the way some writers seem able to easily express themselves in great detail in their writing, while I find it difficult to set down anything more than the essential details. Perhaps this could be partially explained by the fact that during my working career as an engineer, the majority of my writing was confined to the preparation of technical specifications and proposals that must necessarily be confined for the most part to essential facts and figures.

However, I eventually came to the conclusion that this may not be the sole reason for my inability to express myself well in my writing. I felt that perhaps something in one of my past lives might have something to do with it so I decided to investigate this possibility with the help of my psychic contacts.

In response to an e-mail, Wendy James, suggested that Rene Beaupre might be able to help me. It was from his website at: www.luvdragons.ca/rene that I learned that he has paid two visits to the Other Side during Near Death Experiences resulting from lightning strikes and that he feels that he is here to use his talents as a Mystic to help us open our mind to the possibilities of what our future holds, and to show us our sacred life-force which all Humanity and the Universe share for eternity. Rene is located 25 miles from me, in Kanata, one of the western suburbs of Ottawa. When I telephoned him on a Saturday afternoon I found him at home, and I had a really warm friendly feeling while I was talking to him. Although he said that he does not facilitate past life regressions, I made an appointment for a reading. He told me that the main purpose of his work is to help people find themselves in their lives, to gain awareness of their own powers, and to improve their lives by using their natural gifts.

So, in 2005, on the 23rd of November, I headed west. My destination was Rene's home, and when I arrived I found that he lived in an old farmhouse, set well back from the road, at the end of a bumpy laneway. Before his front door was opened I could hear the barking of a dog followed by a man's voice saying, "good dog, don't bark." A slender, bald-headed individual with dark eyebrows, and a white goatee beard opened the door. Rene shook my hand and ushered me in to what he called the "healing room." In beginning the reading, Rene informed me that he was being told that when I am writing and not meeting my self-imposed deadlines, I introduce a fear factor when missing these deadlines that affects my self-esteem.

During this 2005 reading I wanted to acknowledge the help I was getting from the Other Side; in particular, the suggestions I have received from Beulah regarding my description of Eagle Starfire. I told Rene that I thought Beulah might be assuming an appearance to attract our attention; however he told me that her flamboyant dress and long ivory cigarette holder were indeed her normal look.

I was also anxious to tell White Fox how pleased I was that John Bentley Mays, at Humber College in Toronto, had agreed to be my mentor, while I am writing this book, and that I also appreciated the lucid dreams I was having that seem to reassure me that, with help from the Other Side, I will become a better writer. Rene told me that if you ask it will come. "When you are dealing with the paranormal, like comes to like, because there are a lot of unemployed people up there, available to help us."

We next moved on to look at my past lives for evidence of anything that might be inhibiting my writing ability. Rene was able to quickly narrow the search down to the year 1192, at which time he found that I was a bard with a Welsh heritage. In this period, which was prior to the signing of the Magna Carta, any opposition to Prince John was dealt with severely. As a bard, a wandering minstrel or trouba-dour playing a three string musical instrument and singing stories, I could usually be sarcastic and get away with it; however, I clearly became too controversial in what I wrote and sang and was flogged, then dragged and banished to the wilderness as a punishment. After wandering for days in the forest I was finally killed by an animal. This certainly seemed more than enough to make me reluctant to write again. Consequently, this karma could be carrying over to inhibit my writing today.

When I mentioned my friend Bill M. to Rene, he said he was getting an image of a big-faced man with glasses who was laughing. Bill told Rene that the only thing that survived the journey to the Other Side was his sense of humor; with-out it he would be one miserable man. When I mentioned to Rene that I have been trying unsuccessfully to establish an after-death-communication (ADC) with Bill he told me that Bill was rolling over laughing because he has tried so many times. Rene agreed with him when Bill said that I am trying too hard. In addition, Bill also reminded me once again to stay away from decaf because it's not coffee, and said that he wished he could have spent more time with me because he enjoyed my company and our conversations. He said he is still around me, usually in the back seat, when I am driving my car.

Rene then said he could see someone else coming in, someone in an Air Force uniform. I told him that it must be Homer S., my pilot from World War II who had passed over a week earlier. The image of a large four-propeller plane that appeared next was the Lancaster Bomber that Homer flew so well, with our crew of seven that included me as navigator. Homer reported that things are very nice there, but he is sad, but not in a negative way. He is just very emotional right now; he loves me a lot and we will be chatting. When I asked if there was anything he wanted me to tell his wife, Joan, he said he misses her, and he is waiting for her, but meanwhile she still has to get on with her life. He said that he is very grateful and proud of his daughter Rae. She needs a big huggable teddy bear.

I next had a question for my Mother. I wanted to know the time of my birth, so my daughter could prepare an astrology chart for me. Mom said it happened at 11:35 in the morning, back before the days of Daylight Saving Time. She also told Rene that my Dad was reborn in Africa eight years ago.

During this reading, I asked Stu G. if Jim J. is better now that his wife is recovered. They were in a canoe, on a fishing trip, when we dropped in on them. Jim said that he now is content.

Then I asked my Native American spirit guide, Eagle Starfire, if he is in agreement with the writings of Black Elk an Oglala Sioux? He replied, "to a certain degree. The man has a great imagination; he is a good writer but he only has two feathers, not a full head. I learned later that North American Indian headdress often included red cloth, glass beads, porcupine quills and eagle feathers. Such bonnets were the regalia of Plain leaders, whose exploits were numbered in eagle feathers.

There was one member of the Group of Eight Infinite Divine Light that I had not yet contacted. It was Isis, an Egyptian Goddess. Rene reported that she was there, and she is a very profound lady who is known for healing and poetry, as well as fertility.

At one point during this reading we felt a draft move through the Healing Room. This prompted Rene to check to see if the tape recording he was making of the Reading had been erased. Rene later explained that the spirits of the reading were letting us know that high energy was being used throughout the reading. Sometimes that energy can cause problems with electrical machines of all types. It can sometimes also drop the temperature in a room by 20 to 30 degrees.

When the reading was over Rene told me that he would like to "open my hands up more" because he said that once the energy starts to move, the mind would work with it. He did this by asking me if I could feel the ridges of his fingerprints, stroking one finger at a time. When I could, he seemed to transfer energy through that finger to my hand.

I left the farmhouse with a warm, glowing, energetic feeling that stayed with me through the entire drive home. Later that evening I realized that a tight knot of the muscles in my upper back between the shoulder blades, that had previously been troubling me, was no longer there. Also, on the following day, I still felt a warm glow whenever I thought about the Reading. It took me back to how I felt when as a boy, when I was having a particularly severe bout of asthma; my mother took me to a faith healer. That day, when we left the healer's home my asthma had been replaced with a wonderful feeling of energy.

XV.

# Past Life Trio

According to my Blackfoot Spirit Guide, Eagle Starfire, I have had thirteen lives, and through my visits to the Other Side, I have learned that three of them have been of particular interest to me. Rene Beaupre, found that I was a bard with a Welsh heritage who met an untimely death for something I wrote. In addition to that short life, I have been a London Watchmaker and a Navigator on a large Sailing vessel.

Sometimes while I am restoring an antique clock I get the feeling that someone is looking over my shoulder, watching me. I was pleasantly surprised one day, while reading a monthly magazine, published by the National Association of Watch and Clock Collectors, NAWCC, to find that, back in 1726 there was a watchmaker in London with the same name as mine. In a Visit, in July 2002, with Jan as the medium, I was able to talk to him. He told me that he was not a very good watchmaker, but his father had insisted that he be one. He showed up later in November 2004 during a reading with Rene. This time he was upset because I had given the owner of a fine Antique Grandfather clock a new key that would make it easier to wind up the heavy weights in his clock.

William felt that this violated the clockmakers code to always retain the original design. A successful past life regression would perhaps allow me to visit William's watchmaking shop to see him producing a fine pocket watch by hand using his comparatively simple tools.

During this 2004 visit, Rene also briefly saw me as a navigator on a large sailing ship. I found this to be most interesting in view of my wartime experience as a navigator on Lancaster bombers, in the Canadian Air Force, and I would love to go back and relive my life on a sailing ship to see what navigation aids I was using. Was I limited to a compass and crude sextant, or fortunate enough to have a simple marine chronometer for determining longitude? I think it would be very interesting to contrast this with my experience as a navigator during WWII, when our aircraft were equipped with the latest H2S and GEE electronic aids to aerial navigation that, providing the enemy wasn't jamming them, allowed us to accurately determine our position.

As mentioned in the previous chapter, Prince John, whom one historian said "could never miss an opportunity to kick a man when he was down" took a dislike to something I said or sang about him, and banished me from the kingdom. If, with the aid of a Past life Facilitator, I could return to that life and forgive those responsible for my early death, it might prove beneficial today in my present life. I would love to know what the comment or song was that offended him.

XVI.

# Past Life Regression

Past life regression is a journey, usually under hypnosis, which leads to another time and another place that your soul has experienced in the past. The memory of this experience exists in your subconscious mind. Most people take the journey because they are curious, but in my case, I would like to go back to that time in my past where I was killed for writing, and forgive those responsible. Having done that, my writing ability might improve.

Dr. Georgina Cannon, in her inspired book *"Return, Past Life Regression and You"* gives an example of a regression that illustrates the process. Her client Annette wanted to let go of the pain of her childhood years. During her first regression, she found herself a male, 20 years old, with dark skin, in a place where the houses were small and people were working, digging, and men carried baskets on their shoulders. A king appears in a procession and people begin to cheer. The king has a big dark beard and wears a small gold crown. His wife is beside him.

He then finds himself working with the king making plans for a school to be built, so he must be quite important. As an old man, he is a teacher, teaching a large number of children. When he is dying, people come to his home to pray over him, and after his death his body is carried through the town and people are singing.

Annette believed the lesson of her past life was to be kind to people and help them. The wisdom was that love is the most important thing; that we can overcome anything with love.

In December 2005, my son Steve agreed to take me to Barrhaven, to the home of Frances Wyllie, where, by past life regression, I would attempt to go back to my earlier life in which I was killed for writing. When Rene Beaupre gave me her name I thought he had said that Frances was a little old Scottish lady. When I got there I was surprised to find that although she was indeed diminutive, and from "over there" with a pleasant accent, to boot, she was far from old. Since Rene, for some time, had been unable to find her phone number, I told Frances how pleased I was to find her. She led me down the hall to a room with dark blue walls that had a large double sized couch with a soft futon on it. On one wall was a beautiful enlargement of a white wolf that reminded me of my Spirit Guide, White Fox. Beside the couch there was a chair and a small table with an electric kettle and a collection of teas. Frances offered me something to drink, a cup of tea or coffee, or a glass of water, but I declined, until later.

Next, she suggested that I lie down on the couch and make myself comfortable. I laid down on my back as she pulled a white cover over me. Frances began by suggesting that I think of a place in nature that was peaceful that I had been to and would go to again. That was easy for me to imagine since I have a favorite spot by the river that White Fox calls a sanctuary. I ride my bike there, and sit by the water and enjoy the view. I have a rock that I usually sit on and watch to see if there are any fish jumping. Frances proceeded to softly suggest that I use my imagination to relax, starting with my eyelids and moving slowly down my body to my toes. Unfortunately, although she tried twice, she was not able to hypnotize me. This was perhaps because I had some difficulty hearing her and during the second attempt her dog started barking. It was a pleasant learning experience for me though and I now have a better idea of how a regression begins. As I was leaving, Frances suggested that I might try her teacher, Garry Rondeau, who gives a course in Regression at the local community college.

Dr. Georgina Cannon illustrates the difference between a psychic reading and a past life regression in her book "*Return.*" She states:

*"Many clairvoyants can see past lives as they work with a client, but it is important to remember that the interpretation is theirs and not yours! An ethical clairvoyant will suggest that you find a past life regression therapist so that you can personally experience the journey and gain the wisdom and healing it brings."*

Information from a psychic doesn't usually remove symptoms (i.e. writing inhibition). To get resolution you should experience the memory, with its associated emotion, yourself. Your experience of the memory through regression will contain a feeling of "knowing" that a psychic reading cannot convey.

For various reasons including bad weather, it took four attempts before I finally visited Garry's home in early 2006. He is located in Richmond, 30 miles west of me and like Rene Beaupre, his home is also situated well back from the road, behind some large Pine trees. When I arrived, he hung up my coat as I removed my shoes. I found Garry to be a grandfatherly man with a broad smile and bushy gray eyebrows. He led me to a pleasant room that had a large green reclining chair against one wall. Before sitting down, I spent some time admiring the pictures on the walls. As I stood there I felt a powerful surge of spiritual energy in my stomach that reminded me of a similar feeling I had earlier experienced as I was leaving Rene Beaupre's home. It left me with the feeling that the Spirit world wanted me to know that I was on the right track.

We started by discussing my objectives for the session. I told Garry about my suspicion that there might be something in one of my past lives that could be inhibiting my writing ability. I related to him what Rene Beaupre had discovered in an earlier reading; that as a bard or troubadour in 1192, I was killed for something I wrote. We agreed that our primary goal for the session would be to try and go back to that time to resolve this issue.

When I was ready, Garry proceeded by telling me to relax into a deeper peaceful state by imagining a place in nature with a stonewall leading down into a valley with soft green grass. The birds were singing and I could feel the warm sun on my face. Then I was asked to imagine that I was going through a door leading to a long corridor with windows. Through these windows I was able to see myself at different ages, starting as I am today, regressing back to when I was born, and finally ending up in my mother's womb. However when Garry tried to take me beyond there, to 1192, he was unfortunately not able to.

The second time he tried to take me back, I got an image of being in the Arctic, and looking down on a vast area of snow and ice extending as far as I could see. At this point I felt cold in spite of the two covers over me. I was told later that that is a normal condition associated with a trance state.

On the third attempt, I was able to quickly enter a deeper trance. This time I could see a series of stained glass images above me that were continuously rotating. Recognizing that

I was in a deeper trance, Garry tried helping me to access my mind to release my writing inhibition. With his help I told my subconscious mind that I would like to be able to provide more detail when I write.

On the completion of the session I was brought to a fully alert state, and we were then able to review the session. Garry suggested that just before I go to sleep when I am in the alpha state of consciousness, if I visualize being back in 1192 and forgiving the person responsible for my death it might help my writing ability. I realize now that I was expecting too much from a first session with a hypnotherapist, but nevertheless it was quite rewarding.

I received Deborah's name, when a picture fell off a wall in the Rockcliffe home of Pamela, one of my clock customers. The large picture that was hanging beside her 200-year-old family heirloom Grandfather clock, with wooden works, fell to the floor. On the way down it must have hit the old clock, because the pendulum had fallen off. As I was leaving Pamela's home I mentioned that earlier in the week I had been in Richmond to get a past life regression. Pamela said that she had several regressions about six years ago. When I asked for the name of a regression facilitator she came up with Deborah's. Deborah Fish has a part-time private practice for counseling, and hypo-psychotherapy. She provides Health and Counseling Services at Carleton University. If you believe, as I do, that nothing is accidental or coincidental, the two dentals, it is easy to speculate that the reason the picture fell was to lead me to another Past Life facilitator. What made me mention it in the first place? It is certainly a subject that rarely comes up in conversation.

It was early evening during a cold winter's night in March of 2006 when Steve dropped me off at the elderly Medical Arts building in the center of town. My anxiously awaited appointment for a regression with Deborah Fish was for 6:00 p.m., and in the Waiting Room, I half expected that I might get another surge of spiritual energy similar to the one I received during my visit to Garry Rondeau, which would reassure me that I was on the right track, but this time nothing like that happened. When Deborah opened the door to welcome me in to the next room I met a young woman with a beautiful broad smile and long fair hair. She led me to a sofa with large soft pillows. After explaining to me that you never know who or what you are going to get during a regression, she started by helping me to relax, with the help of some soothing music in the background. Deborah was obviously quite expert as a Past Life Facilitator. She tried several times to take me back, without success. An hour later, we finally had to give up, after deciding that the anti-seizure medication that I am taking was probably interfering with the regression. This was hard to deal with since I was so looking forward to going back and reliving my past lives. I am almost tempted to temporarily stop taking my medication and try again. Particularly, when I suspect that the seizure I had undergone in October 2005, may have been a one-time thing that marked the start of my new lifetime.

XVII.

# Children Who Remember Past Lives

In another of his wonderful books *"Life After Death, The Burden of Proof"* Deepak Chopra tells us that child psychologists are aware that there is a critical period, usually between infancy and eight to ten years old, when some children seem to remember past lives. They report making decisions about their next lifetime, once they got to heaven, choosing a new family and new challenges.

Some very young children between two and five begin speaking of their past lives–spontaneously, without hypnosis or prompting. Some even as young as two and still in diapers blurt out, "I remember when I died before" or "My other mommy had curly hair". They often describe details that they have had no way of learning in this life. Such memories happen naturally to young children in all countries of the world, regardless of the beliefs of their parents. It can happen at any time to any very young child, but parents often fail to notice it because they don't realize it's possible or don't know what to look for.

For thirty-seven years, Dr. Ian Stevenson traveled the world from Lebanon to Virginia investigating and documenting more than two thousand children's past life memory cases. In his book *"Old Souls,"* Tom Shroder, the first journalist to accompany Dr. Stevenson in his fieldwork, follows Stevenson into the lives of children and families touched by this phenomenon. Shroder interviewed a woman that told him that when her daughter was not yet two, the little girl stood at the top of the stairs looking down on her reflectively for a few minutes, then said, *"I'm glad I chose you."*

We must not remain deaf to this. In *"Children's Past Lives"* Carol Bowman tells parents that it's important not to make fun of a child when he or she talks about his or her past life, because then they will stop talking about it. If there are fears left over from the previous life, those fears that the child is not encouraged to talk about can become phobias, or irrational fears, like her son's fear of loud sounds. Such fears can go on through a person's life and can interfere with their being able to live life in a normal way.

Bowman tells us that past-life memories, unlike fantasies, were related by children in a matter-of-fact way and remained consistent, even over long periods of time. She also looked for behavioral traits, such as phobias or personality twists, which had no ostensible origin in the current life and often disappeared when the past life was related by the child and accepted by the parent. The phobias of her own children had shown her how this took place, and her book is filled with fascinating accounts of remissions of such difficulties.

The emotional maturity with which toddlers relate facts from adult lives—and even tell of their deaths—indicates that something extraordinary is happening. These children have much to teach us. Past life memories related by children is a phenomenon with far-reaching implications for every person who wonders about their own past lives.

XVIII.

# Scientific Evidence

How do I know it's true? When my Mother tells me that my Father has been reborn and is now an eight-year-old boy in Africa, can I believe it? I certainly can't prove it! What if the skeptics who support the "ashes to ashes" viewpoint are right?

In the late Fifties, Bill M. and I had the privilege of working beside scientists at Bell Labs in New Jersey. It was the main research and development arm of the United States Bell System. At its peak, Bell Labs was the premier facility of its type, developing a wide range of revolutionary technologies, including the transistor, laser and information theory. While there I developed an appreciation of the scientific method that uses a body of techniques for investigating phenomena and acquiring new knowledge of the natural world, as well as the correction and integration of previous knowledge, based on observable, empirical, measurable evidence, and subject to laws of reasoning. All this evidence is collectively called scientific evidence.

Using similar techniques to these, Dr. Gary E. Schwartz, Ph.D., presents scientific evidence of life after death in his book "The Afterlife Experiments." Daring to risk his international academic reputation, he and his research partner Dr. Linda G. Russek, asked some of the most prominent mediums in America to become part of a series of extraordinary experiments to either prove or disprove the existence of an after-life. He is a professor of psychology, medicine, neurology, psychiatry and surgery at the University of Arizona and director of its Human Energy Systems Laboratory; his credentials include a doctorate from Harvard and a professorship at Yale - an impressive background he carefully lays out at the beginning of the book.

The point is to show his intention of approaching the subject with objectivity and scientific scrutiny. His intent at the outset was not to prove or disprove the existence of life after death, but to determine whether the successes that many mediums claim, could stand up to the scientific method. Working with Dr. Russek, Schwartz devised experiments that, as best they could, would eliminate the possibility of cheating or fraud of any kind. They were able to enlist the cooperation of such well-known mediums as John Edward, Suzanne Northrup and George Anderson, who to their credit, placed no conditions on the experiments; they would participate exactly as directed by the scientists.

The early experiments were conducted much like John Edward's "private sittings," if you've seen his popular TV show "Crossing Over with John Edward." In this situation, the medium sits facing a "sitter," whom he or she has never met, and proceeds to apparently receive information from a deceased friend or relative of the sitter. The medium is often able to relay initials, names, dates and specific incidents relevant to the sitter and the deceased. In Schwartz's tests, each medium had a session with the same sitter, and the experiment was repeated with several sitters. The sitters were instructed to reply to any questions from the mediums with either a yes or no, with no elaboration. All "messages" from the deceased were carefully recorded.

How well did the mediums do? The results showed that the mediums ranged from 77 to 95 percent accuracy! But is this proof of contact with consciousness that exists after death? Or are the mediums just good guessers? Similar experiments were conducted, but this time with students, who have no claim to psychic abilities, acting as mediums. They were able to achieve only 36 percent accuracy.

So are the mediums just better at it, or are they experts at doing "cold readings," as the skeptics suggest, taking clues from the sitters' voice inflections and body language. To eliminate this possibility, Schwartz and Russek's experiments became more and more stringent, to the point where the mediums were not allowed to see or even directly hear the sitters. All answers were relayed to the medium through Schwartz. Even with the tightest controls, the mediums' accuracy was above 90 percent. The book provides loads of data, complete with bar graphs and charts that show that the mediums were highly accurate in conveying messages that were specifically meaningful to the sitter-deceased relationship.

But what does it all mean? Does it conclusively prove that consciousness survives death? Although it seems clear from the text that Schwartz is fairly convinced that it does, as a scientist he stops short of saying that the data evidence leads absolutely to that conclusion. But it sure is compelling. You really have to read the book to appreciate how compelling some of the mediums' hits are - information so specific and so unlikely to be guessed through cold reading, that we have to consider that something extraordinary is taking place. But what? Are the mediums reading the sitters' minds? (This might be discounted because the mediums were sometimes able to relay information that was unknown to the sitter at the time, but was later confirmed through research.) Are the mediums tapping into the collective unconscious? Or are they contacting the dead? Even the mediums say they don't know how it works. But Schwartz considers all of these questions and more, and provides carefully thought out responses.

Two of the most interesting chapters of the book are "Answering the Skeptics" and "Looking Forward and Outward." In the former, Schwartz presents questions typically posed by skeptics and then answers them based on his findings from the experiments. In the latter, he states 11 ways in which the mediums might seem to succeed - from fraud, cueing and lucky guesses, to memory in the universe and actually talking to dead people - and then offers what skeptics speculate about them, what mediums say about them and what the experiments actually reveal. Regarding "talking to dead people," Schwartz says, "The data appear to be as valid, convincing and living as the mediums, sitters, skeptics, and scientists themselves."

Fascinating also is the chapter that examines the question of how our lives might change if it were conclusively proven that human souls live forever - how it would change our daily lives, how we interact with people, how it might affect our legal system, marriage vows and more. The effects would be profound and pervasive.

"*The Afterlife Experiments*" is an important book about some very important research - important because it's the first unbiased, controlled examination of the phenomenon of spiritualism. Its research that we hope will be continued by Schwartz and taken up by other research teams.

XIX.

# Skeptical Professionals

Some of my friends are eye rollers. That's the reaction I get when I tell them about my 'visits.' They roll their eyes, look at the ceiling, and quickly change the subject. I find this to be particularly true when talking to professionals such as doctors, scientists, and fellow engineers. The bottom line in science is a solemn commitment to the evidence obtained through the conduct of valid, controlled and replicated experiments.

According to a poll conducted for Maclean's magazine by sociologist Dr. Reginald Bibby at the University of Lethbridge in June 2006, 62% of those polled believe in heaven and Angels, while 46% believe we can communicate with the dead. Almost half of the people you meet then are potential eye rollers.

At one time I too was a confirmed eye roller. When Bill M. passed over to the Other Side in 1983, it took me fifteen years before I tried to confirm his belief that we can communicate with the dead. Although I tried to keep an open mind, because of my engineering background I was not able to convince myself that it was possible.

In his remarkable book, "Reinventing Medicine", Dr. Larry Dorsey writes:

*"I used to believe that we must choose between science and reason on one hand and spirituality on the other, in how we lead our lives. Now I consider this a false choice. We can recover the sense of sacredness, not just in science, but in perhaps every area of life."*

I find that I too can now relate to and endorse Dr. Dossey's new belief, because for me the dichotomy no longer exists.

Upon graduating with honors from the University of Texas at Austin, Dr. Larry Dossey, worked as a pharmacist while earning his M.D. degree from Southwestern Medical School in Dallas, 1967. Before completing his residency in internal medicine, he served as a battalion surgeon in Vietnam, where he was decorated for valor. Dr. Dossey helped establish the Dallas Diagnostic Association, the largest group of internal medicine practitioners in that city, and was Chief of Staff of Medical City Dallas Hospital in 1982.

In his book, *"Reinventing Medicine"* Dossey writes, *"I once felt differently. I believed that if nonlocal mind were valid, "killer experiments" could be done that would be so persuasive they would sweep away all opposition and quell every argument. This reflected my view of science -- that scientists are completely rational creatures who, when faced with data, respond as objectively as a computer and "do the right thing." I no longer believe this, because I have learned that my idealized image of science was wrong. Scientists are not unemotional computers. They can be as biased and ornery as anyone else, particularly when venturing outside their field. As one respected scientist said when asked to review a scientific paper dealing with nonlocal mental events, "This is the sort of thing that I would not believe, even if it were true."*

# XX

# Encouraging Dreams

The first thing I do, following my morning prayers, is record my dreams from the night before in my Dream Journal. When I have a dream that I feel is significant I mark it with a large asterisk to simplify finding it again.

If you go to Google, enter Dreams and hit Search, you will get close to 258 million hits. Such notables as Sigmund Freud and Carl Jung are listed, but in my opinion, the best source by far, for information about dreams, and their interpretation, is Sylvia Browne's *"Book of Dreams."* By dividing dream experiences into five categories she makes it easier to interpret them. All three of the following dreams fall into a category that Sylvia calls "Information or Problem Solving Dreams."

The first dream is one that for me was quite extraordinary because I got to see my Spirit Guide, White Fox, giving me a thumbs-up! In one of my visits to the Other Side on November 18, 2004, he said that he was waiting for me to share my message with the world, and he would let me know when I was on the right path with a vision or dream. Three nights later when I had decided to proceed with my book, I had a lucid dream where I arrived at a motel to find that the front door was locked. There was a man standing behind a glass door, with a smile on his face, pointing his finger towards me and nodding his head as if to indicate approval of what I was doing. On my next visit I thanked him for the confirmation dream, to which he replied "Definitely."

On May 10, 2005, I dreamt that I was at a school function, feeling left out, when a very nice lady said she would help me. She left me with a wonderful feeling of unconditional love that gave me a warm, comfortable and contented sensation. I believe that she was Beulah my Specialized Helper offering to help me with my book. I hesitate to say for sure because on previous visits she was described as looking like Tallulah Bankhead, but it does confirm my suspicion that she originally adopted this appearance and behavior to attract our attention and ensure that we noticed her. She has since proven to be helpful with my book.

My third dream was during the night of March 18, 2006, when I dreamt that I was in a room with several people when the door opened and a voice said "Move over and make room for Bill Westbrook's teachers."

Following each of these remarkable dreams I felt that I was receiving encouraging confirmation that I was on the right track and getting help with my book from the Other Side.

# XXI

# Three of a Kind

I find it intriguing when I consider the way groups of three have come my way since I unwittingly entered the phenomenal paranormal world at that Psychic Fair in 1998. In eight years, I have received readings from three mediums, had three noteworthy dreams, identified three of my past lives worth pursuing with the help of three past life facilitators, and enlisted the aid of three travelers in the fifth dimension.

Using their psychic gifts to receive the higher frequencies of the spirit world, the mediums have been able to help me visit the Other Side. Janet Remington was the first of the three mediums that have come into my life beginning in 1998. She was the one who introduced me to the paranormal world, and reunited me with my long time friend, Bill M. That was the highlight of her reading for me. During that first reading Jan told me that I had "a lot of writing to do" with an "army of guides" on the Other Side, who would be helping me. At the time, I had no way of knowing what that meant. However, at a later visit my brother-in-law Alf told me that I have a "platoon" of people over there that are helping me.

Later my Mystic friend Rene told me "it is not surprising, because there are a lot of unemployed people over there."

During the following five years until 2003, Jan gave me yearly telephone readings from her home located two hundred miles from me. Her readings were made up of three parts; Tarot Cards, Tea Leaves and Clairvoyant. Using cards and tea leaves she would give me predictions of upcoming events in my life for the year ahead. Using her Clairvoyant skills Jan would then take me to contact my loved ones on the Other Side. Since it seemed to me that the majority of Jan's predictions did not materialize, I came to prefer dispensing with the cards and leaves and going directly to contact loved ones on the Other Side.

My association with Jan as a Medium ended in 2003 when she moved to the States, and my Internet search for another Medium led me to Deborah Levin, in Toronto. Testimonials on her website by some of her clients were very positive, and when I contacted her she readily agreed to answer the questions given in Appendix A, on "Choosing a Medium." Deborah told me that at age five, she started to have psychic visions. Now she is able to see past (retrocognition), present (clairvoyance) and future (precognition) events. Deborah has been listed in Chatelaine Magazine in their "Who's Who of Canadian Women" and was voted "the Best Psychic in 1999", by Toronto's Now Magazine in that year.

My first reading from Deborah in April 2004 went very well. Seeming to be quite professional and sensitive, she told me that I would write a book that is spiritual in nature that will be well received around 2007. According to her I will have a very long life.

A year later, an Internet search for a Medium closer to Ottawa led me to my third Medium, Wendy James, who lives on a nearby farm. After checking her website, I called her and made an appointment to see her at an upcoming local Psychic

Fair. When I arrived at the fair, I found Wendy to be a pleasant fair-haired young woman with a broad, friendly smile.
In spite of the somewhat distracting background noise from
the Fair, I found her reading to be quite perceptive. During
the reading, White Fox told me to forget my self-imposed
deadlines; that information flows freely through me, and all
my Spirit Guides are with me –"a houseful."

As I mentioned before, with regard to the dreams recorded
in my journal, over these eight years, there were three events
that I feel were significant. One was meeting my Spirit Guide,
White Fox, and his indicating that he approved of my starting this book, which was very exciting for me. Seeing the
nice lady, at the school function, who may have been Beulah,
left me with a warm feeling; and finally the dream with a
clear voice stating "move over for Bill Westbrook's teachers"
strengthened my resolve to proceed with this book.

On 6 Aug '03, during one of my visits, I encountered a
trio of Bills. In addition to my faithful friend, Bill M. who is
always there for me, there were two more Bills; Bill C. who
was the owner of the Tea and Coffee Company I worked for
during my summer vacations from high school and he also
sang in the choir at our church. He suggested that I think of
him as a grandfather who was spiritual rather than religious.
Finally there was Bill G. who was my old friend from the
local Clock Club. At the time I had several French Carriage
Clocks on my bench. When I asked him which one he liked
best, without hesitation, he picked the large one on the right
that I favored as well.

XXII.

# Pencils and Typewriters

When Susy Smith got a letter from her mother, who had been dead for six years, she was understandably excited, or as she says in her book "*the Afterlife Codes*" she was "floating on her own personal warm fuzzy cloud." The letter arrived by means of 'automatic writing' via the pencil she was holding. Her hand just wrote by itself without her conscious will being involved in any way. The writing, which ran scragglingly across the page in run-to-gether words, said, "I am your Mother and I love you." That was the first of many messages she received.

Then one day, Susy's typewriter talked back to her. She had been trying to type up a description of her efforts to contact her mother. At a loss for words, she slumped in her chair to relax, letting her fingers rest lightly on the typewriter keys. When she said aloud, "I wish I knew what I was talking about," her hands began to type slowly, seemingly of their own volition. What was written was quite different from what she had intended. The writings are contained in Chapter 19 in her book, "*the Afterlife Codes*," titled "Mother's Chapter," which Susy believes was written by her mother, using 'automatic typing.'

Reading her book we learn that Smith is convinced that she will be able to provide conclusive proof of life after death, with the activation of what she calls her afterlife codes when she dies. Prior to her death she deposited a certain coded phrase in a computer, with the intention that after she dies, she will transmit this code to a living medium that will compare it with the computer's version. When they match, surely this should be incontrovertible scientific proof that the soul survives physical death, for who but Susy Smith could have known her code. Smith has offered a $10,000 prize to anyone who can successfully receive her secret message.

On February 11, 2001, Susy Smith, had a massive heart attack during dinner and passed away. She was 89 years old. To date, the reward has not been claimed.

Chico Xavier was Brazil's most respected medium, a position of great moral authority in a country where an estimated 20 million people believe in spiritism - a type of Catholicism based on telepathic communication with souls of the dead. Brazil has the world's largest spiritist population, and, in a career spanning 75 years, Xavier became its most important figure. Even though barely educated, he published more than 400 books–the spirits of dead people supposedly dictated the texts to him telepathically. "*Poetry From Beyond The Grave*" (1932), for example, contained 259 poems revealed to Xavier by 56 dead Brazilian poets, including some famous ones. In 1981 and 1982, he was nominated for the Nobel peace prize.

Skeptics consider automatic writing to be little more than a parlor game, although sometimes useful for self-discovery and for getting started on a writing project.

XXIII.

# Meditation

I have been meditating for years, with mixed results because of my uncertainty as to what I should expect from it. Recently however I received a guided meditation CD, included in a wonderful little book called "Meditation, Achieving Inner Peace and Tranquility in your Life" by Brian Weiss M.D. With his soothing voice this CD works really well for me. He starts by telling me that *"At first focus on your breathing. Let it be nice and deep and even... relaxed yoga breathing. This is the way within."* I find that this CD helps me relax and quickly enter the "Twilight Zone," that occurs between waking and sleeping, known as the alpha level. At this level we are in an altered state of awareness that provides access to the subconscious mind where the incredible total body of knowledge of all our previous lives resides. Following a suggestion from Garry Rondeau, I make a statement to my subconscious, when I am at that level that: *"I am overflowing with creativity that flows freely into successful writing, and all is empowered by the White Light of the Holy Spirit"* When I do this I am in effect my own hypnotherapist, and if I am successful, I should be a better writer.

When it comes to meditation, the Dalai Lama is an expert. He tells us that: *"The very purpose of meditation is to discipline the mind and reduce afflictive emotions."*

Meditation is a way to balance a person's physical, emotional, and mental states. It has been used as an aid in treating stress, anxiety, pain management, and as part of an overall treatment for other conditions including hypertension and heart disease. In *"Same Soul, Many Bodies,"* Brian Weiss states:

*"We can use meditation to resolve personal conflicts and difficult relationships or to help the heart to heal. But eventually for all of us the primary purpose of meditation is to achieve inner peace and balance through spirituality."*

### ACCORDING TO DEEPAK CHOPRA:

*"Meditation has only one reason: to get in touch with your soul, and then go beyond that and get in touch with the consciousness that your soul is a ripple of. It might be a good stress management technique, but there is only one real purpose, which is the means to enlightenment." Many individuals have claimed to reach a state of enlightenment, including many famous yogis and meditation masters from well-known spiritual traditions. Mahatma Gandhi was said to be an enlightened seeker of truth. Siddharta Guatama, the Buddha, was also said to have reached the "ultimate state of enlightenment" or "nirvana.*

# XXIV

# Suicide

Once a month, I meet for lunch, at a local Chinese restaurant, with fellow retirees that I worked with at the telephone company. At a recent lunch, the man sitting beside me told me that he had lost his son and the man across the table said that he lost his daughter, both of them by suicide. As a parent, I don't know how I could ever recover from such a traumatic experience. But Canadian studies show that approximately 16 percent of adolescents contemplate suicide in any given year. However despite these statistics, suicide remains a taboo subject, and for the suicidal youngster's parents, shame often leads to silence.

According to Statistics Canada, except for car accidents, more young Canadians die from suicide than by any other cause. Most of them suffer from depression or other mental disorders, and most are male. The associated morbidity chart gives "intentional self-harm" as the official cause of death for 527 people aged ten to 24 in 2002.

Each year as Christmas draws near, TV stations begin re-airing Frank Capra's *"It's a Wonderful Life"* in which a character, portrayed by Jimmy Stewart, decides against suicide after having been persuaded by his Guardian Angel to remember the good he has been able to do during his lifetime. The incidents related in "*It's a Wonderful Life*" take place at Christmas, and this was probably simply done to heighten the warm feeling of the story, in fact suicides do not peak at Christmas, although many news stories suggest the connection. Suicidal tendencies arise in people at all times of the year for either real or imaginary reasons.

Life today tends to be more stressful, and people today are continually challenged with worries about survival. We are also often harassed by employment, financial, emotional or health concerns, it is not uncommon for people to feel suicidal at least once in their lives, with thoughts such as-- *I would be better off dead!*

Suicide is the 11th leading cause of death in the United States and is also very common, among older people. As approximately every 83 minutes, one adult 65 years of age or older, commits suicide in the United States. These tend to be very violent deaths with 8 out of 10 suicidal men over the age of 65 using a gun to kill themselves. Statistics show that in many countries elderly people kill themselves at a higher rate than any other segment of the population. Physicians, nurses, and other health care professionals should be alert to the possible threat of suicide in elderly patients with chronic illness, particularly in patients with multiple illnesses, symptoms of depression, or other suicide risk factors. By identifying those seniors at higher risk of suicide, interventional measures can be initiated that may prevent deadly actions by such people.

At the root of this problem lies the fact that before you can love others, you must first learn to love yourself. In this society, we're taught that praising ourselves is selfish and wrong. But praising ourselves for things that are good about ourselves only helps us. It is a healing thing to do, something that nourishes our self-worth. When we love ourselves, we're happier and more true to our own selves... and that happiness and ability to be free spreads to others. We all are here to learn to *love*. One of the first lessons we are trying to learn is a love of ourselves. Once we have achieved such unconditional love of self and others we become enlightened and can then live in nonjudgmental harmony with our fellow human beings. Despite the fact that depression is a mental condition and can be effectively treated in 90% of the cases with a combination of medication and therapy, unfortunately, only 1 in 3 people with depression will get help.

Low self-esteem is a condition that is prone to foster ideas of self-destruction. A person with low self-esteem sees himself as worthless because he feels he contributes nothing to the community. He thinks that the world would be a better place without him. There are also some who are terminally ill and don't want to go through the pain and suffering of a slow and painful death, who contemplate or actually commit suicide.

Just like the heart, liver or kidneys, the brain is an organ of the body that can become sick. Chemicals in the brain, called neurotransmitters, regulate how people think, feel and act, thus the brain can become sick if these chemicals are out of balance or are disrupted, and the illness called clinical depression can result.

When a person takes his own life we are told by advanced Psychic Mediums, Sylvia Browne and James Van Praagh, that one of the first things the suicide victim realizes is that he is not dead. He has an overpowering feeling of being very heavy because the earth ties are still part of his essence. His soul remains stuck between the physical and the spiritual worlds. The soul feels guilt, and anguish for a life cut short. He learns how significant his life would have been if he had stayed alive. He senses the grief and anger of those he left behind. The unhappiest situation is that he finds himself in a limbo state. He is stuck in "no-man's-land" with the constant memory of his horrendous act. Anyone who takes their physical life neither lives nor dies; instead the spirit resides between the earth and the spirit worlds until the time of its normal passing (the time that the body would have passed over if death had not been self-inflicted). This state—not really dead or alive—is a terrible condition of existence. When a suicide occurs, a soul must return and go through another lifetime under the same or similar conditions, and relive and learn the experience again.

It is not only terminally ill people with physical pain who consider suicide; there are also those with a fear of losing control, and perhaps, a deep concern that they will lose their freedom of choice. Also they may want to save their loved ones expense and/or anguish by committing suicide.

At present, in North America, there is no acceptance that life-prolonging treatments in late life degenerative conditions can be inappropriate. A number of ways of dealing with such hopeless situations have emerged, all of which involve either withholding or withdrawing various forms of treatment. Some of these are exercised by the patient and include refusal of treatment and patient-executed "do not resuscitate" orders.

It is possible to live with a terminal illness yet experience very little pain. Doctors agree that for 85 to 95 percent of people, pain can be controlled, so in the caring community provided by a Hospice, it is possible to die with dignity and enter what some have called the Through the Looking Glass environment, compared with the high-tech nightmare that has all too often been our society's accepted approach to death.

# XXV

# Last Visit

On 8 June 2006, I turned off my laptop and cleared my desk in readiness for a one hour phone Reading with Deborah Levin in Toronto. I had decided to have one more visit before completing my book, and had prepared a list of ten people I hoped to contact on the Other Side. Some of those on the list were loved ones of friends who had questions they wanted me to ask when I got there. Although competent mediums are quick to point out that they can't be sure who they will see on any visit, Deborah was able to contact all ten of the departed on my list.

When contact was established Bill M., was there, as usual. Deborah said he was shaking his head in amazement that he knew an author. He said that I deserve a pat on the back, and that I don't give myself enough credit for what I have accomplished. Bill's wife Betty had some family matters relating to relatives in Western Canada on which she wanted me to get his opinion. He readily answered her questions and also told her to put herself first and not to be so accommodating. I then asked Bill what made him think that we don't need a medium. His reply was that it was just common sense. When I enquired if he had been able to make an After Death

Communication without a medium, he changed the subject. I had a question for my Mom, about my Father. Previously she told me that he had been reborn eight years ago in Africa, and I was curious to know his whereabouts there, and his gender. She was busy at a social function but had time to tell us that he was a male in an African country beginning with an E with a skin color that is East Indian.

Grandmother Westbrook was faint, because she is moving on to a higher level. She said that she is going to refer a new guide to me who will reveal information to me about weird omens or symbols. Not sure why I would want that, maybe my next book, but I will have to wait and see.

My brother-in-law, Alf, was there. He was very worried about something to the point of being almost overwhelmed. When he was here, we enjoyed similar hobbies. I asked him how he liked my 54-gallon corner aquarium, with the big Discus fish. He said that he often drops by to admire them. When I questioned him on what hobbies he had there, he told us they were musical and artistic. He said that he was being pushed to draw or paint. When he was here he was very good at both of those activities.

My pilot from Air Force days, Homer, was there. When we told him that his wife Joan loves him and misses him he said that he knows, but when he was asked if his Mother and brother were there with him he seemed to be more connected to his living family members. He doesn't feel that they can cope. Deborah told him that he should back off a bit and conserve his energy.

Maria was the wife of my watchmaker friend from India. Anthony wanted to convey to her how much he and his son Peter loved and missed her. In life, she was a well-educated High School teacher that spoke several languages. She was there and although she seemed to hear and understand me, she responded rapidly in another language.

We told Flora S., that her husband Herb, who was a fellow member of the Bible Class, thinks about her all the time and how much her grandkids enjoy having her stop the rain, on their request, when it is falling. When Deborah first connected with her she got a real rush of raised spiritual energy that usually indicates an advanced soul. Flora is totally fine and comfortable and quite enjoying her return to the spirit world.

My mentor John Bentley lost a friend, Brian P., who passed over suddenly a year ago. He wondered how Brian was doing and whether he was "rambling around" there? Deborah found that, before he left, Brian had a terminal illness that he was stoically hiding. Initially, he said he found getting around there to be difficult, but he is now becoming a lot more comfortable. He said that he is a slow learner in the Spirit World, but he expects to be rambling around later.

Knowing that there is no time over there, I wondered what my old friend and member of the local Clock Club was doing at his leisure. Deborah said Bill G., was there, sitting at a large table with a disassembled clock movement that was spread out over the table, and a watch that he was working on with a pair of tweezers. I asked him what he thought of the 200-year-old Grandfather clock, with a wooden movement, that I had ticking away beside me. He was amused and said they were fussy and a lot of work to repair. Knowing that Bill drove an Alpha Romeo when he was here, I enquired what he was driving there. He showed Deborah an image of a vehicle like a Hummer that he surprisingly said he loves.

When I told the father of my son's partner, Reg F., how much we loved her, he said he knew that. He said he was doing OK. At first he missed everyone and felt guilty about leaving his wife, but is now feeling good. I always hesitate to call someone and tell them that I was able to contact one of their loved ones on the Other Side. I don't know how they will take it. However in this case when I telephoned his daughter, Linda, she was very pleased to hear from me, and called me back later to tell me that she had just realized that the day of our contact was her father's birthday.

When I asked Deborah to thank my Spirit Guides and Angels for all their help with my book she said that they were all cheering excitedly. They told her that I must go on and finish it.

Beulah showed up, still looking like Tallula Bankhead, with her long cigarette holder, to tell me that I must complete the book. She said that she didn't have much time for writing when she was in the theatre.

During this session I told Deborah, as I mentioned earlier, that I suspected that my epileptic seizure was triggered to let me visit the Other Side while I decided what my goals would be during my extended lifetime. Seizures happen when a surge of electrical energy passes between cells in a person's brain. Deborah told me that the electrical jolt of the seizure transformed my life in a way that presented a challenge that is a gift. She also told me that she was seeing four colored boulder-like objects that seemed to represent my goals in my extended lifetime. They were blue, amber, red and green. She said that I am very close to accomplishing the blue one, by writing this book. It will be published in the Fall of 2007. Using her gift of precognition, Deborah described the woman I will meet in Church who will help me get it published.

Before I hung up the phone, I thanked her for using her paranormal gifts to help me, once more, visit the Other Side.

## Mixed Blessing

During our discussion Deborah told me that my seizure in October 2005 was a gift; a blessing of sorts. But a godsend isn't necessarily all good; sometimes there may be drawbacks. For example, the doctor who attended me in the ER had to notify the Ministry of Transportation that I had suffered a seizure, so soon after that, my Driver's Licence was suspended for a year. Although the lack of mobility gave me more time for writing, the anti-seizure medication prescribed by my neurologist had several nasty side effects. It affected my balance such that I could no longer take the enjoyable bike rides, down by the river, to spend time at the sanctuary that White Fox likes. An additional drawback was that the anti-seizure medication seemed to prevent me from having a past life regression.

## CHANGING ATTITUDES TOWARD DEATH AND DYING

Americans are taking a new approach to the issues of terminal illness and death. A survey conducted by the Roper Organization for the Florists' Transworld Delivery Association (FTD) revealed a widespread openness to discuss these previously taboo topics.

There is perhaps no subject more difficult to talk about than dying. Yet, the vast majority of respondents (86%) believe that people are more open today in talking about serious, terminal illness than in the previous 10 years. The subject of death itself is open for discussion, notes Kathleen O'Neil, Roper vice president: *"A majority of respondents [67%] say they personally can talk about death and dying and do so with more ease than ever before."*

Three-quarters of those surveyed believe that support services provide an excellent way to help people endure the death of a loved one; with women (81%) being more likely than men (71%) to agree. Approximately one-third (36%)

have used a support service or would avail themselves of one in the future.

The support services currently gathering the most attention are hospices, which provide a variety of care to terminally ill patients and their families. One of the fastest-growing segments of the health care industry, there are nearly 2,000 such facilities in the U.S. In 1992, 210,000 Americans chose hospices over traditional hospitals for their final days.

XXVI.

# Dying with Dignity

Like most seniors, when I reach the end of my journey, and the time comes to head back to my eternal home on the Other Side, I hope to die a quiet death here at home, in the presence of my loved ones, but the fact is that millions don't get their wish. Today, many experience death and dying amidst dazzling technological advances. By the 1950s, social trends were changing and most people died in hospitals rather than in their own homes. This change reflected the growing number of treatments available in hospitals. The medical profession increasingly saw death as a failure. Cancer was the most feared diagnosis. Physical pain afflicted at least three quarters of cancer sufferers and appropriate painkillers were rarely used. Morphine was considered addictive and too dangerous. In founding St Christopher's Hospice, in London, England, in 1967, Dame Cicely Saunders made an extraordinary contribution to alleviating human suffering. In the mid 1960s, when palliative care was in its infancy, Dame Cicely rejected the prevailing orthodoxy that suffering was an inevitable part of terminal illness. With her colleagues she pioneered another way. A holistic approach, caring for a patient's physical, spiritual and psychological well being, marked a new beginning, for the care of the dying. Her legacy is the UK hospice movement, which leads the world. A principal aim of hospice is to control pain and other symptoms so the patient can remain as alert and comfortable as possible. Hospice services are available to persons who can no longer benefit from curative treatment; the typical hospice patient has a life expectancy of six months or less. Hospice programs provide services in various settings: the home, hospice centers, hospitals, or skilled nursing facilities. Patients' families are also an important focus of hospice care, and services are designed to provide them with the assistance and support they need. Dr. Balfort Mount, at the Royal Victoria Hospital, in Montreal, coined the term "*palliative care*", (from Latin *palliare* – to cloak or cover) in 1975, so that one term would be acceptable in French and English as he brought the movement to Canada. Both hospice and palliative care movements have flourished in Canada, and internationally. Palliative care programs developed primarily within larger healthcare institutions, while hospice care developed within the community as freestanding, primarily volunteer programs.

Patients who enter a hospice program can receive services either at home or in a hospital or nursing home. Typically, aggressive medical treatments are stopped but medicines are routinely administered to ease pain and to improve the quality of life. In addition to nursing care and the daily services of a home-health aide, hospice patients can be given massages, acupuncture or back rubs. They also receive visits from social workers who try to help them express their feelings and review their life experiences and from spiritual counselors who try to help patients prepare for death on whatever terms the patient desires. Hospice gives patients the time to say four things to their family, 'thank you, please forgive me, I forgive you and goodbye." Personally, when my time comes, I will readily agree to enter a hospice program. Unfortunately, though, there is a critical shortage of these wonderful programs.

## LIVING WILLS

My Last Will and Testament has an attachment, a type of Power of Attorney that appoints my wife as my 'attorney for personal care.' It gives her and my family the authority to make any personal care decisions for me that I am mentally incapable of making for myself. In effect it instructs them that if I am brain-dead to "pull the plug" of any machines that artificially prolong my dying process.

Similarly a Living Will, sometimes called an advance health care directive, is a specific type of power of attorney in which the signer requests not to be kept alive by medical life-support systems in the event of a terminal illness or coma, including if you wish, the decision to refuse intravenous feeding or turn off the respirator if you're brain-dead–should you become incapable of making that decision. A Living Will could also specify whether you want to donate your organs when you die.

Some experts say Living Wills are highly flawed, because they are too general to be useful and are not always followed. Many others agree that, Living Will or not, end-of-life planning should always include a document that designates a specific person to be a health-care proxy: someone who can make decisions for a person should he or she become incapacitated.

The documents that set out your wishes for medical care may go by various names depending on where you live: advance directive, living will, directive to physicians, medical power of attorney, patient advocate designation, and so on. These are all terms for health care directives -- that is, documents that let you write out instructions about the type of health care you want to receive, including who should over-see your treatment if you are unable to speak for yourself.

Personally, I am adamant on these issues. When my time comes, at the end of my current journey, here on earth, I would like to ensure that there are no delays, since I prefer a more comfortable, shorter life, using the least possible medi-cal intervention.

Until recently, Living Wills had no legal status in Canada. They could only provide advice to family members and doctors, which might or might not be acted on. But most provinces now have, or are planning, legislation, that gives them legal force.

Many people make use of a Living Will because they do not wish to endure any pain or suffering if weakened by a fatal disease. They want to "die with dignity," so that family members will not have to go through the emotional pain of watching their loved one sleep through many years of life with no response to any stimuli. This form of death is known as passive euthanasia, where death is not inflicted with drugs, but is allowed by cutting off life support.

In the Northern Territory of Australia the Rights of the Terminally Ill Act was a controversial law legalizing euthana-sia within that Territory. Passed by the Territorial Parliament on May 25, 1995 the Act allowed terminally ill patients to commit medically assisted suicide, either by the direct involvement of a physician or by procurement of drugs. It required a somewhat lengthy application process designed to ensure that the patients were both mentally competent to make the decision and in fact terminally ill.

The passage of the bill – one of the first of its kind in the world-provoked a furor in Australia, and indeed in much of the rest of the world. The Act received both widespread sup-port from "death with dignity" groups who saw it as model to be followed elsewhere, and widespread condemnation from euthanasia opponents who sought to overturn it.

The Northern Territory proved to be unwavering in its support for the proposal, and its repeal did not appear to be in sight. However support in the rest of Australia was much weaker and opponents began turning to the federal Parliament, demanding it nullify the law. On March 25, 1997, the federal Parliament did so, passing the Voluntary Euthanasia Laws Bill that amended the Northern Territory's Charter with the provision that the Territorial Legislature no longer has the power to pass laws legalizing euthanasia.

While the law was in effect, four people committed suicide through its provisions. An additional two had received approval to do so when the law was nullified; a proposed amendment to the Voluntary Euthanasia Laws Bill allowing them to proceed did not pass.

Dr. Philip Nitschke, executive director of Australia's national dying with dignity organization, Exit International, assisted the first of the four to commit suicide. He visited Toronto recently to attend a global conference of right-to-die organizations, and while there reported that group members have taught themselves the chemistry to make a 'suicide pill;' an illegal lethal barbiturate whose main component is amylobarbitone. He estimated that people would need to invest only about $425 to manufacture sufficient amounts to kill themselves. About 100 are said to be on the waiting list.

In the Netherlands, patients and potential patients can specify the circumstances under which they would want euthanasia for themselves. They do this by providing a written euthanasia directive. This helps establish the previously expressed wish of the patient even if the patient is no longer able to communicate. However, it is only one of the factors that is taken into account.

In Switzerland, there are several organizations, which take care of registering patient decrees, forms that are signed by the patients declaring that in case of permanent loss of judgment (e.g., inability to communicate or severe brain damage) all means of prolonging life shall be stopped. Family members and these organizations also keep proxies, which entitle its holder to enforce such patient decrees. Establishing such decrees is relatively uncomplicated.

## Ethical Wills

Ethical wills go back to Biblical times. Today, there's renewed interest in leaving heirs a testament of values. Although ethical wills vary widely in content, people who write them usually relate what they value most in life. They often express love for their survivors and tell them not to grieve. Some explain past actions or recount formative events. Many dispense advice. An example is a now-deceased doctor who wrote that he regretted giving up medical research for a more lucrative career as a surgeon. "There's no greater compensation than being happy in your work," he wrote to his children. Ethical wills are not legally binding, but many attorneys encourage clients to write them as codicils to their regular will. They help with estate planning, says James Carolan, a trust and estates attorney in Port Huron, Mich., because they clarify "what's important and what they really want to do with their money." The wills also allow attorneys to personalize clients' legal documents by, say, incorporating text that indicates the motivation for setting up a trust.

XXVII.

# At the End

Following my seizure, Deborah Levin, a medium I respect, told me that I am going to have a long life. When my time does come to pass over to the Other Side, I will no doubt have mixed feelings. It will be sad to leave family and friends here, but I will be looking forward to returning home on the completion of my current Journey.

Knowing what is waiting for me, I have no fear of death. Naturally, I prefer that my last days here be relatively painless, but I have confidence that nowadays it is possible to live with a terminal illness, yet experience relatively little pain.

If necessary, I would readily agree to enter a hospice program. I would like no delays, since I prefer a more comfortable, shorter life, using the least possible medical intervention. I wish to donate my organs, following cardiac arrest.

After cremation of my body, I would like my ashes to be spread over a lake in Algonquin Park, in Ontario.

XXVIII.

# In Closing

Well there you have it. You may have had a hard time believing that all those things could have happened to one person in such a relatively short time. To tell you the truth, looking back on it, I have a problem with it myself.

Little did I realize, during my reluctant visit to that Psychic Fair, back in 1998, that it would lead to visits of quite another kind? Visits that, for me, would open up a new paranormal world that I had no idea existed. Meeting my first medium, Jan, and with her help, my friend, Bill, on the Other Side, was a deeply life-changing experience for me. An experience that confirmed the existence of an afterlife, and led me to a changed perspective and a new nonjudgmental outlook on my life and those around me.

Why me? What have I done to deserve this special treatment? Why was I granted an extended lifetime? Why did White Fox take over as my Spirit Guide and convince me that I should write this book. There must be a lot of people out there that are better writers than I am. Maybe he was listening when Jan told me "I don't like sitting still for a minute and am a patient, methodical individual that looks for the gold in situations and usually finds it." Although he tells me that I can do anything, I certainly need a lot of help from my friends. Fortunately, I have been blessed with many; both here and beyond the veil.

What about the trios? I have used three mediums, had three noteworthy dreams, identified three of my past lives worth pursuing with the help of three past life facilitators and enlisted the aid of three travelers in the fifth dimension. I admit that when I recently wanted to have a new driveway installed, here at my home, I deliberately asked three contractors to bid, but I did not deliberately do that with any of my trios, they just happened. Rene tells me that this reflects the triple aspects of life as in "Life, Death and Rebirth," and the Holy Trinity; Father, Son and Holy Spirit.

Should you decide you would like to contact loved ones on the Other Side, I think you will find that most mediums are sincere, and want to give you the best reading they can. Although I usually prefer to meet a medium in person before my first reading I have found that telephone readings can be quite successful.

Rest assured that there is an afterlife to return to, on the completion of your current journey, here on Earth. There is no reason to fear a painful death as you return to your beautiful Home, where your loved ones await you.

May you have good health and peace of mind as you continue on your current journey through life while doing the best you can with who you are? Be assured that your Guardian Angel and Spirit Guides, on the Other Side, are watching over you, and helping you on your way. As we part, I send you unconditional Shambhalan love.

XXIX.

# Epilogue

## 14 JANUARY 2007

I went to the Ottawa Spiritualist Temple for the first time and enjoyed hearing the playing of the organ that took me back to my boyhood at Dufferin Presbyterian in Toronto. A medium that was sitting beside me told me that I am surrounded by many Spirits who want to thank me for what I have done. Carole-Anne Bosley a Medium friend who was there as well told me that someone in the military was saluting me for something I had done. This had to be my pilot, Homer S., from WWII, who appreciated my consoling his wife, Joan, following his recent passing over to the Other Side.

## 18 FEBRUARY 2007

While back again at the OST, a visiting minister from Toronto told me that she saw a woman in the Spirit World that was sick for a long time and could not speak to me then, wanted to say hello. My sister-in-law Jeannie W. was a MS patient in Toronto at the Providence Centre before she passed over to the Other Side. In the final stage of her illness she was unable to speak.

Before the service started at the Spiritualist Temple, Reverend Sigrid Sommer told me that there was a man with me in the Spirit World that wanted me to know that although I do not always know the way here on Earth, when the time comes he will show me the way Home. With Bill M. in the back seat I sometimes get lost when driving. This must have been him.

### 29 MARCH 2007

Lately it seems that whenever I am in a hospital I get a wonderful feeling of confidence that results when I look at myself in a mirror. I think it could be White Fox encouraging me to continue on my current track reassuring me that I can do anything. When I left the elevator on my way to see Dr. Skinner, my neurologist, I looked out the window, up into a beautiful blue sky where I saw a vapor trail from a plane that was flying straight up toward heaven. Dr Skinner told me that following two seizure-free years we could slowly taper off the anti-seizure medication. If successful I should then be able to ride my bike again.

### 29 SEPTEMBER 2007

During my first visit to the Other Side my blonde Spaniel pup "Buddy" apologized for being so hard to control many years ago. When I noticed a little dog like him in a nearby car soon after I decided to write my book I thought it could be a sign from the Other Side that I was on the right track. The last time I had talked to White Fox he said that he was fond of Buddy and was patting him at his feet.

On 29 September 2007, my book was finally finished. I went to see a man who was separating from his wife and had some photographic equipment for sale. When I rang his doorbell he opened the door and reached down to prevent a blonde cocker spaniel puppy just like Buddy from getting out.

Last Visit with Deborah Levin (2 October 2007)

As usual Bill M. was there. After all, he was the guy that got me into this in the first place. Deborah said that he was just laughing. When I told Deborah that although Bill is convinced that we don't need a medium, he can't seem to contact me she said that her contacts with the Spirit World are usually visual not audible When I mentioned that my phone sometimes rings, with no one there, **she said it was Bill!** That explains why he has been so amused. He had picked a very appropriate way for a phone company engineer to give a sign to a friend back on earth. Too bad it took me so long to catch on. I was at the point where I was considering having our phone number changed. While shaking his head he says I am unstoppable and wonders what I will do next?

Thanking all those helping with my book including White Fox, a Specialized Helper named Beulah, and all the others Deborah said that some of them had gone on to help others.

When we asked my Mother if she had a message for my sister, Olive, she said that Olive should get control of herself and do what is best for her. Although he is no longer in the Spirit World, Deborah saw that my Father was indeed in Ethiopia as a young boy with a prominent white man possibly as an adoptee.

As a joke we asked Bill G. the time? He said that he was still just tinkering with watches and clocks although we both know that there is no time there.

I was anxious to know if I will have another seizure if, with the help of my Neurologist, I reduce my anti-seizure medication. Deborah said I won't have another seizure, but I could reduce the dosage and not stop altogether.

When I asked her if I will write another book she replied that I would write another that had a different non-fiction style. Could be represented by another of the colored boulders from a previous reading. Time alone will tell.

## 8 OCTOBER 2007

It is Thanksgiving Day here in Canada. We have been blessed with unusually mild weather. As predicted by my Spirit Guide, White Fox, my book will be published in the Fall of 2007. As I finished typing I had a feeling that someone was looking over my shoulder when the phone rang. There was no one there, but guess who it must have been?

APPENDIX

# Finding a Competent Medium

The three mediums and a Mystic that I have used up to the point of publishing this book have proven to be quite gifted at what they do. To enable us to make a visit to the Other Side, without dying or experiencing a NDE, we need the assistance of an accomplished and reputable medium to provide the link between the two worlds. If you are hoping to communicate with loved ones on the Other Side, then a medium is the one to call. If you want a reading to be mostly about *your* life, see a psychic, astrologer, or tarot card reader. Sources of information about reliable mediums in your area include word-of-mouth, Spiritualist Churches, Psychic Fairs, New Age Bookstores and Internet Web Sites. I have found the Internet to be a useful resource for this purpose. By searching the Web for mediums in my area I have found several. If they have a Web Site, you can review it to gain a first impression of their suitability.

There is an Internet web resource at: www.bestpsychic-mediums.com that is provided by Bob Olson, who, like me, was a cynical skeptic until he met his first genuine medium. On his website he provides descriptions and contact information for some of the most gifted psychic mediums in the United States.

Finding a suitable medium is important. As in any occupation, you will find people that range from highly gifted to those who are not talented. Regrettably, there are fraudulent mediums that take advantage of people who have lost a loved one who they are anxious to contact. However, most mediums are sincere and only want to give you the best reading they can.

Carole Lynne, in her book, "*How to Get a Good Reading from a Psychic Medium*," suggests the following "good questions" to ask a prospective medium:

1. What kind of reading do you do?
2. What do you call yourself? A psychic? A medium?
3. Do you use any tools in your readings, such as, tarot cards, runes or crystals; how do you use them?
4. What do you consider the main purpose of your work?
5. What should I expect to get out of the type of reading you do?

A typical satisfactory answer for #5 is the following:

"What you should expect is that I will not deceive you, that I will tell you just what I see and nothing more... that if I do not have a message or do not see anything, that I will be honest with you about that. I think that clients should approach each psychic consultation with an open mind and an open heart and not limit the experience with too many expectations at all... other than integrity and honesty from their chosen psychic."

He or she should welcome questions; if not, find someone that will. Remember not to tell the medium anything about yourself, when you make an appointment. A professional medium does not want to know anything about you.

Just ask questions about the reading and give your name and phone number. Prepare a list of what is happening in your life, including what prompted you to find a medium?

In her book Carole Lynne offers straightforward, plain talk about what mediums can and can't do, and how to prepare to get the most out of an encounter with the Other Side. Her wise counsel is: trust yourself. You are the one who knows best what a reading means in your life. Carole has a web site at: www.carolelynne.com.

It is advisable to get a reading from someone who concentrates on one type of reading. Some readers can do several types of readings, but it is better to stick to one type at a time. I find that a tape recording of a reading can be useful. For a live reading the medium will usually provide a tape. On a telephone reading I prefer to use my tape recorder and a speakerphone.

XXX.

# Suggestions for Further Reading

Conversations with God, Books 1, 2 and 3, Neale Donald Walsch

An uncommon dialogue

G.P.Putnam's Sons 1995, 1997 and 1998

The Secret of Shambhala, James Redfield

In Search of the Eleventh Insight

Warner Books 1999

A Course in Miracles

Text

Workbook for Students

Manual for Teachers

Foundation for Inner Peace

A Return to Love, Marianne Williamson

Reflections on the Principles of a Course in Miracles

Harper Collins 1992

Everyday Grace, Marianne Williamson

Having Hope, Finding Forgiveness, and Making Miracles

Riverhead Books 2002

The Wheel of Life, Elisabeth Kubler-Ross, M.D.

A Memoir of Living and Dying

Simon & Schuster New York 1997

Life on the Other Side, Sylvia Browne

A Psychic's Tour of the Afterlife

Dutton 2000

Blessings from the Other Side, Sylvia Browne

Wisdom and Comfort from the Afterlife for This Life

Dutton 2000

Talking to Heaven, James Van Praagh

A Medium's Message of Life

Dutton 1997

One Last Time, John Edward

A psychic medium speaks to those we have loved and lost.

A Berkley Book 1998

How to Get a Good Reading from a Psychic Medium, Carole Lynne

Get the Most Out of Your Contact With the Other Side

Weiser Books 2003

The Afterlife Experiments, Gary E. Schwartz, Ph. D.

Breakthrough Scientific Evidence of Life After Death

Pocket Books 2002

The Truth about MEDIUM, Gary E. Schwartz, Ph. D.

Extraordinary Experiments with remarkable psychics

Hampton Roads Publishing Co. 2005

The G.O.D. Experiments, Gary E. Schwartz, Ph. D.

How Science is Discovering God in Everything Including Us

ATRIA Books 2006

Return, Dr. Georgina Cannon

The Healing Power of Your Past Life Regression

OHC Publishing 2004

Messages, George E. Dalzell, L.C.S.W.

Evidence for Life after Death

Hampton Roads Publishing Co. 2002

We Are Eternal, Robert Brown

What the Spirits Tell Me About Life After Death

Warner Books 2003

Hello From Heaven, Bill Guggenheim and Judy Guggenheim

~After-Death Communication-confirms that life and love are
        eternal~

Bantam Books 1995

Final Exit, Derek Humphry

The Practicalities of Self-Deliverance and Assisted Suicide for the
        Dying

Dell Publishing 1991

Embraced By The Light, Betty J. Eadie

"A Most Profound and Complete Near-Death Experience"

Gold Leaf Press 1992

One Last Time, John Edwards

A psychic medium speaks to those who have loved and lost

Berkley Publishing Group 1998

The Book of Reincarnation, Sirona Knight

How your past lives may influence you today

Barron's Educational Group 2002

Inspiration, Dr. Wayne W. Dyer

Your Ultimate Calling

Hay House Inc. 2006

Reinventing Medicine, Larry Dossey

Beyond Mind-Body to a New Era of Healing

HarperCollins Publishers 1999

Getting a Life, Copthorne Macdonald

Strategies for Joyful and Effective Living

Hounslow Press

the Afterlife Codes, Susy Smith

Searching for Evidence of the Survival of the Soul

Hampton Roads Publishing Company 2000

Destiny of Souls, Michael Newton, Ph.D.

New Case Studies of Life Between Lives

Llewellyn Publications 2000

Journey of Souls, Michael Newton, Ph.D.

Case Studies of Life Between Lives

Llewellyn Publications 2002

Many Lives, Many Masters, Brian L. Weiss, M.D.

The True Story of a Prominent Psychiatrist, His Young Patient, And
        the Past Life Therapy that Changed Both Their Lives

Simon & Schuster Inc. 1988

Same Soul, Many Bodies, Brian L.Weiss, M.D.

Discover the Healing Power of Future Lives Through Progression
        Therapy

Simon & Schuster, Inc. 2005

Mirrors of Time, Brian L. Weiss, M.D.

Using Regression for Physical, Emotional, and Spiritual Healing

Hay House, Inc. 2002

Meditation, Brian L. Weiss

Achieving Inner Peace and Tranquility in Your Life

Hay House, Inc. 2002

Living Our Dying, Joseph Sharp

A Way to the Sacred in Everyday Life

Hyperion, 1996

How To Know God, Deepak Chopra

*The Soul's Journey Into the Mystery of Mysteries*

*Harmony Books 2000*

Life After Death, Deepak Chopra

The Burden of Proof Harmony Books, 2006

Children's Past Lives, Carol Bowman

How Past Life Memories Affect Your Child

Bantam Books, 1997

Old Souls, Tom Shroder

Compelling Evidence from Children Who Remember Past Lives

Simon & Schuster 1999

ISBN 142515197-3